STAYING HEALTHY
IN SICK
ORGANIZATIONS:

THE CLOVER
PRACTICE™

KATHLEEN A. PARIS, PhD

Staying Healthy in Sick Organizations: The Clover Practice™

This publication is based on the author's personal experiences with a variety of organizations. The author is not engaged, however, in rendering legal, psychological, medical, or financial advice to individuals.

If legal, psychological, medical, or financial advice or assistance is required, the services of a competent professional who can focus on the reader's individual situation should be sought.

ISBN: 1-4392-0120-X
ISBN-13: 9781439201206
LCCN: 2009903058

Visit www.booksurge.com to order additional copies.

In Memory of My Father, Vincent L. Paris

ACKNOWLEDGMENTS

Many people have encouraged me in the writing of this book. The following have been particularly inspiring and supportive. My deepest thanks to:

Pat Alea
Gabrielle Banick
P.J. Barnes
Joanne Berg
Maria Brunette
Carol Gosenheimer
Karen Grede
Darin Harris
Liz Menzer
Carolyn Mewhorter
John Poparad
Gloria Pursell
Don Schutt
Consuelo Springfield
Hazel Symonette
Nancy Thayer-Hart
Ann Zanzig

Also, my sincerest thanks and love to my family.

Kathleen A. Paris, PhD
Madison, Wisconsin

TABLE OF CONTENTS

INTRODUCTION:
THE CLOVER PRACTICE™

It's a funny thing—When people hear the title of this book, they get a knowing look in their eyes. They know what I mean when I talk about sick organizations.

Most modern workplaces are at least a little bit sick in my view. They are sick because they are designed and managed according to obsolete principles. They are sick because too many people without appropriate skills and motives supervise other people. And willingness to maintain illusions keeps them sick. Sick organizations are like sick people. They spend an awful lot of time trying to treat their symptoms.

What about your work situation? Think about how you feel at the end of your work day or your shift. Now imagine yourself leaving work feeling peaceful. That is the peace of mind The Clover Practice™ can give you. The Clover Practice™ is for anyone who

- Works for a paycheck
- Is willing to take responsibility for his or her own actions
- Wants to go home after work feeling peaceful

If this describes you, welcome! Get comfortable and read on. It doesn't matter if you don't supervise anyone or if you supervise hundreds of people. It doesn't matter if you work in corporate America or city government or for the biggest university or the smallest school. It doesn't matter if you own your own business or work as a contractor. The Clover Practice™ can help you maintain your integrity, honor, and emotional health even while working in organizations with major design flaws.

I like to make things simple. In my consulting practice, whenever I help a client solve a problem, I use three principles that have become The Clover Practice™. I urge my clients to use the practice as they wrestle with problems and I use it to guide my own behavior. I hope it will be your guide also and "…something to hold in our minds in moments of confusion and doubt."[1]

This is the The Clover Practice™:

1. Tell the Truth, Always
2. Speak For Yourself
3. Declare Your Interdependence

A practice is something you do all the time, no matter what the circumstances. The Clover Practice™ will become second nature to you. You will have ways to deal with circumstances that stump you now. The principles themselves are not necessarily new, but living them as a whole package probably is. The principles are explained in detail in Chapters 1–3.

I use the common three-leaf clover as the symbol for this practice. Green is the color of life. A clover is a living thing—and the whole point of working is to sustain our lives. The three-leaf clover is symbolic too because each leaf is important. With one leaf missing, it's not a three-leaf clover anymore. Similarly, the three principles in The Clover Practice™ are meant to be used together. They reinforce each other to help you stay healthy emotionally.

The Clover Practice™ is simple, but definitely not easy to live. No one can live this practice perfectly, but everyone can strive to. I believe that if you are willing to learn what the three leaves of the clover mean and use them as a guide—you will be able to stay emotionally healthy in most work situations. This means doing the job you are getting paid to do without it tearing at your spirit or leaving you feeling diminished as a person. The Clover Practice™ can also help you connect with people you work with in a positive and mutually supportive way. We don't have to wait for other people or "the system" to change to have healthier work lives ourselves.

To me, staying healthy at work means you can go home at the end of the day or at the end of your shift feeling peaceful. It means you can stop thinking about work and enjoy your life. (There are the dramatic situations that make it hard to forget about what happened at work, but these shouldn't happen every day or even every week.) Some occupations are, by their nature, dramatic, such as medicine, law enforcement, firefighting, etc. For those in high-stress occupations, The Clover Practice™ can help reduce the drama we create ourselves.

Many workplaces are saturated with fear. I don't want you to be scared anymore. Every day so many of us go to jobs where we feel afraid—afraid of our bosses, afraid about how we are doing, afraid to speak up, afraid to tell the truth. Some of our fear is well founded and some of our fear is our own creation. By picking up this book, you have taken the first step to conquering the fear inside your own head and taking control of your own life.

What is emotional and mental health? Even the surgeon general of the United States says in a recent report that mental health is not easy to define because every definition reflects particular values.[2] A dictionary definition of mental health is, "A state of emotional and psychological well-being in which an individual is able to use his or her cognitive and emotional capabilities, function in society, and meet the ordinary demands of everyday life."[3] By my definition, mentally and emotionally healthy people:

- Know their boundaries—what is theirs to do, worry about, and control. (This implies that they know what is not their business as well.)
- Are helpful—they have enough satisfaction in their lives that they can reach out to other people. There's enough water left in the well to share.
- Are hopeful—they have a positive outlook and generally assume that good things will happen. When bad things happen, they try to see past them into a more positive future.

- Are peaceful—they seek to live calmly in the moment without worrying excessively about the past or the future.

It is my hope that The Clover Practice™ can help all of us move toward this view of mental and emotional health. Although The Clover Practice™ is focused on keeping your mind and emotions healthy, your physical health will improve if your stress is lower. Our mental, emotional, spiritual, and physical health are very closely tied together, more connected than many people (even some doctors) realize.

I have consulted in public and private, profit and nonprofit organizations. There are more similarities than difference in the experiences of people who work in these varied settings. Public and nonprofit organizations are modeled right after their money-making cousins and catch the same illnesses. The questions for you to answer ultimately will be

- How sick is the place where I work?
- How can I stay healthy?
- Do I need to get out?

You may recognize, with the help of The Clover Practice™, when you are in an environment that is so toxic that you must get out. If you think you are in this situation, go right to Chapter 6.

The three-leaf clover is awfully close to a four-leaf clover, which is synonymous with good luck. Staying emotionally healthy while you work is not a matter of luck, but of intentional choices on your part—decisions about how you act as well as decisions about where you work. Most people have more employment choices than they think they have. You can read more about this in Chapter 6. And speaking of choices, many of us have never made conscious choices about what values, beliefs, and lifestyles we want for our own adult lives. Many of us have not stopped to ask ourselves how what we experienced as we grew up may be affecting our work lives right now. You can do your adult homework in Chapter 4.

The Clover Practice™ illuminates the high road. This practice is not for everyone, only those people who want to be emotionally healthy and peaceful while making a living. Those who have their sights set on control, prestige, and wealth at any cost probably won't get much out of The Clover Practice™.

My hope is that The Clover Practice™ will become your touchstone, helping you stay healthy in your own inner space—your mind, heart, and spirit—while working for organizations that are fundamentally unhealthy. In Chapter 5, I say more about why I believe organizations are more likely to be sick than healthy.

I divide my own career into two halves—pre- and post-1990. I had my career success post-1990 after I figured out that The Clover Practice™ was the way to go. It is my beacon every single day. I offer it to you and guarantee that if you take the time to read about the principles and think about them, the place you work will never look the same and you will have new ways to deal with work in a healthy way.

Some people might think The Clover Practice™ is too simplistic or naïve. As Buddhist monk and teacher Robert Aitken puts it, "Do you think this is naïve? Maybe so, but look where sophistication has brought us."[4]

A bonus of The Clover Practice™ is that it will serve you just as well in your home and family life as it will at work. Imagine a family where everyone tells the truth, where people speak for themselves, leaving the door open for other views and feelings, and where family members rely on and support each other in a framework of interdependent relationships. The more you live The Clover Practice™ at work, the greater will be your ability to use it at home and vice versa.

By the way, this book is written for Americans working in America. I don't know how well The Clover Practice™ plays in other countries. The book will make more sense if you read it in chapter order, but if you're like me, you will start from the back anyway.

CHAPTER 1:
TELL THE TRUTH, ALWAYS

Bella DePaulo, a University of Virginia psychologist who studies lying, says that in her twenty years of research, only one person has ever said he didn't tell lies, but "he was lying," she adds.[5]

In my early career, I was willing to be honest with bosses, colleagues, direct reports, and customers only up to a point. My biggest concern was how something looked. If it looked like I was being totally honest, that was good enough for me. I cringe when I think of some of the things I did and said when I was thirty-something.

I will never forget the day when I heard another person—a consultant speaking at a conference—telling about a situation where she had lied to a client. This was in the days before e-mails and fax machines. She had said a project was finished and ready to put in the mail when it really wasn't. (And the client, unfortunately, offered to come right over to pick it up!) I stood stunned in the back of that crowded room—here was another grown-up ADMITTING that she had lied at work. I thought only I said things were almost done when they were just getting started, or subtly suggested that someone else had caused a delay when I was the one who was behind. This brave speaker said that it was only by being totally honest that we could be healthy and successful in our work. I recognized instantly that what she said was true. That day changed my life.

That is how the first leaf of The Clover Practice™, "Tell the Truth, Always," showed itself. "Always" is significant, because we must tell the truth even when it's not convenient and even when we don't look too good. Truthfulness to others is the only way to stay true to yourself and vice versa. And people who have that kind of deep integrity earn the trust of others, which almost always leads to success.

Truth Is Hard to Find in America

Mainstream religions support honesty and we have a national parable—George Washington and the cherry tree—about telling the truth. In court, people swear to tell the truth, the whole truth, and nothing but the truth. The reality in our society, however, is that dishonesty is OK and even expected. It starts at a young age. How old does a kid have to be to learn that the toy is never as big or as much fun as it looks on the cereal box or on TV? As consumers, we know we are being lied to regularly and skillfully by advertisers enticing us to buy things. We are so accustomed to these advertising lies that we don't even seem to mind anymore. How many of us believe that four out of five dentists recommend anything?

A few statistics help make the point:

- 57 percent of office professionals report that they have been asked (or have seen someone else being asked) to lie for their bosses[6]

- 93 percent of 40,000 workers admit to lying habitually and regularly in the workplace[7]
- College students admit that at least 70 percent of their excuses for missed assignments are lies[8]

Vice President Cheney's chief of staff, Scooter Libby, was convicted of lying to a jury and obstruction of justice in March of 2007. Another top-ranking member of the George W. Bush administration thumbed his nose at traditional views of truth. In an interview with *New York Times* journalist Ron Suskind,[9] the Bush advisor said, "We're an empire now, and when we act, we create our own reality. And while you're studying that reality—judiciously, as you will—we'll act again, creating other new realities...."

News stories abound about companies that boldly lied with terrible consequences for people and the earth we live on. In 2001, Enron, then America's seventh largest company, "dissolved into worthlessness in an ugly morass of accounting fraud and human greed."[10] The collapse left investors empty handed and 21,000 employees out of work, their pension fund gone. Company executives were later found guilty of criminal behavior ranging from insider trading to deceptive accounting, manipulating energy markets and bribing foreign governments.[11]

We have coal and electrical groups paying PR companies to "reposition global warming as theory (not fact)."[12] We have marketers pitching junk food directly to children.[13] We have pharmaceutical companies using PR to define new diseases in order to create a market to match their drugs.[14]

I recently ordered a book that took me by surprise. The title suggested that I could prevent other people from lying to me. I liked the idea of inviting honesty from others. Instead, I found a psychologist who recommended telling elaborate lies to trick other people into exposing their lies. Come on!

Philosopher David Nyberg claims that lying is instinctive in humans and "that life without deception is not possible."[15] He has plenty of examples to point to of individual and corporate lying and deception.

Choosing a Different Path

Morrie Schwartz says in *Tuesdays with Morrie,* "…If the culture doesn't work, don't buy it. Create your own."[16] You can choose to live your life differently. Each of us has control of what we do and say. You can create a culture of truthfulness around yourself, around your desk or machine or classroom. The best part is that it's contagious. Human brains are constructed so that we learn behaviors almost subconsciously from how others behave. You can be more powerful than you ever thought, just by sticking to the truth.

If you are willing to Tell the Truth, Always, you will be trusted by others. If you have a reputation for honesty and integrity, you are more likely to be entrusted with important and interesting work. Eckhart Tolle, in *A New Earth: Awakening to Your Life's Purpose,* says, "Those few people who…function from the deeper core of their Being, those who do not attempt to appear more than they are but are simply themselves, stand out as remarkable and are the only ones who truly make a difference in this world."[17]

> *The desire to be perfect or look perfect is the wish to be God. And that is a sin.*
>
> – Peter Block[18]

Consultant Tom Sant says when people are desperate, they have two choices: improve their situation or resort to lies and deception. For some people, lying and cheating look easier than fixing the problem. But, he adds, what goes around comes around and sooner or later others (inside and outside of the organization) catch on and eventually know whom not to trust.[19]

Nan De Mars, international consultant on office ethics, tells the story of a person who did something unethical at the bidding of her boss. She did what she had been told to do because she was afraid to say no. The irony was that after that incident, her boss never trusted her again. He knew that she was willing to be deceitful.[20]

People lie usually for one of two reasons: to make themselves look better or to protect someone else. In a 1996 study by Bella DePaulo and colleagues, 147 people ages 18-71 kept diaries of the lies they told over the course of a week. According to participants' diaries, only one in four lies was told to protect another.[21]

Even though lying is as common as rainwater, when we lie, we pay a price, even if we are not found out. The people in the study of lying conducted by DePaulo and colleagues admitted to having feelings of discomfort and diminished closeness in the conversations in which they lied.[22]

Telling the Truth, Always, requires both

- Telling the truth to yourself
- Telling the truth to others

They are mutually reinforcing. Often people who find it easy to deceive others just as easily delude themselves.

Most importantly, if you Tell the Truth, Always, you will never need to be in hiding. You will never have to fear that something you said will be found out. You need never worry that you told two people two different things and that they might compare notes.

Research even suggests that you will get sicker less often if you are committed to being open. Honest communication boosts your immune system. One researcher found that people who spoke openly and honestly about stressful experiences or wrote about them (being honest with themselves) not only had lower blood pressure, they also showed souped-up immune systems. Their bodies literally made more white blood cells than the bodies of people in the control group.[23]

The truth is a very powerful force that cuts through the darkness of denial and illusion. It cuts to the core of an issue and illuminates it.

– Eileen R. Hannegan[24]

Following the practice of Telling the Truth, Always, you can leave work with the lightness that comes from knowing that everything you said and did, even if not perfect, was honest and honorable.

The Truth as We Know It

When a witness swears in court to tell the truth, the whole truth, and nothing but the truth, he or she is presumably promising to tell "the truth." We know that the testimony of two different witnesses can be contradictory even though both people believe they are telling the truth. AA and Al-Anon, organizations that have helped millions of people, are founded on the necessity of telling the truth *as we know it*. Those last words, "as we know it," make all the difference. In their wisdom, AA and Al-Anon recognize that it's the best anyone can do.

I may think I know "the truth," but reality may be something else. Have you ever looked at one of those 3-D pictures where it looks like one thing, but if you look at it in a certain way, a different image emerges from the background? Just because you can't see the picture buried in the pattern, doesn't mean it's not there. You can say you don't see it, but you can't correctly say that it's not there.

Hannegan says that speaking the truth means speaking from an inner confidence "that does not require validation and buy in from others."[25] I have learned in my consulting work that if I make it clear that I am speaking from my own point of view, based on what I have heard and seen, and that I am willing to entertain additional information, then I can tell the truth as I see it without getting kicked out.

Being clear that you are speaking from your view of the situation (versus speaking an eternal truth) also makes it easier for other people hear what you are saying.

If you have read anything by Peter Senge, then you know about mental models.[26] These are the views we carry about how the world works, what reality is all about, how things are. Mental models exist in our own minds, developing over time mostly through our life experiences. Everything we see, hear, feel, taste, experience, is interpreted by and filtered through our mental models. What makes mental models so powerful (and difficult to change) is the fact that they are unconscious. We don't know we have them.

One of ten principles of "enlightened business" suggested by Buddhist monk and former diamond company executive Geshe Michael Roach in *The Diamond Cutter* is to "convey true impressions." He says that complete honesty means "the impression which your words leave matches the impressions you have in your mind."[27] In other words, the outside matches the inside. Lying, says Roach, is "giving someone else an impression which does not strictly correspond to the impression that you yourself have of the same thing."[28]

Conveying true impressions is the best we can do when it comes to telling the truth. Karen Grede, a gifted family therapist in Madison, Wisconsin, who specializes in families with troubled teens, likes to get the whole family involved in therapy sessions—parents, grandparents, brothers and sisters, aunts and uncles—everyone in the family who is willing to show up. Grede says that in such therapy sessions, "there are as many truths as there are people in the room."

Psychologist Margaret Wheatley describes the work of theorist Karl Weick who says that we participate in the creation of our organizational realities. Wheatley says, "There is no objective reality; the environment we experience does not exist 'out there.' It is co-created through our acts of observation, what we choose to notice and worry about."[29]

In most workplace situations, there simply is more than one truth about any situation. This is a concept that workshop participants sometimes get upset about. Once a person got red in the face and sputtered, "Are you telling me there is no such thing as 'the truth'?" To which I answered, "People can be involved in the same event and have very different experiences." Each experience is true for that person. Awareness that we construe everything through our own personal lens and that everyone else is doing the same thing frees us up. It allows us to say, "This is what it looks like to me. What does it look like to you?"

We need humility and compassion when comparing realities with other people.

Telling the Truth, Always, or Flapping Your Gums?

Imagine a workplace where people said out loud everything that was passing through their minds. Work would surely cease. How does this comically tragic scene square with "Tell the Truth, Always"? Here's where the line is drawn—I don't have to share my opinions on every topic. They are only my opinions, not eternal truths. My dislike of my colleague's ratty jeans on casual Friday is my opinion and I don't have to share it. This changes, of course, if my colleague asks me if I think the jeans look bad. Then I am compelled to honestly say that I think they look pretty beat up for our office.

An example of the difference between Telling the Truth, Always, and yet not sharing all my opinions is this. I tell the truth if I say that I saw one employee punch another employee in the lunchroom today. But my views on whether either is a worthy husband is my opinion, based on my ideas of marriage and partnership. I don't have to share my opinion on everything.

Table 1.1. Rotary International Fifty-Year-Old Ethics Test

The Rotary Four-Way Test

Of the things we think, say, or do:

1. Is it the TRUTH?

2. Is it FAIR to all concerned?

3. Will it build GOODWILL and BETTER FRIENDSHIPS?

4. Will it be BENEFICIAL to all concerned?

The Clover Practice™ mirrors the same commitment to truthfulness as Rotary International's Four-Way Test for speaking and acting.[30] The Four-Way Test shown in Table 1.1 has been translated into more than a hundred languages.

Sometimes it's hard to figure out whether something is my personal opinion or a truth that must be spoken. The line can be thin. Here are some additional questions to help clarify whether you need to talk about something:

- Will my comment add value?
- Will my comment help me or others get the job done better?
- What are my motives? (See Chapter 2 for more on motives.)

The absolute threshold for speaking out honestly at work is when you believe a negative consequence will befall any of the stakeholders if you do not speak up—customers, clients, patients, workers, visitors, etc. And remember, you are giving your own "true impressions" and need to be willing to accept that you might be wrong. Table 1.2 suggests a dozen ways to Tell the Truth, Always, at work.

Table 1.2. A Dozen Ways to Tell the Truth, Always (At Work)

1. Admit when you haven't finished (or started) a task that is due

2. Admit when you don't know how to do something and ask for help

3. Admit when you do have information, but are not at liberty to share it

4. Refuse to say that someone is "at a meeting" or "gone for the day" when he/she is not

5. Refuse to cover up information affecting the health and well-being of others

6. Refuse to repeat "misinformation" (something you know is not true)

7. State your honest reaction to an idea or proposal, no matter whose it is

8. Give a performance appraisal that is accurate based on what you have heard, seen, and experienced

9. Refuse to distort information about other companies' or organizations' products or services to win business for yourself

10. Admit when you have made a mistake and make any corrections that you can—sooner rather than later

11. Chose the right time and place to tell your truth

12. Describe problems/situations accurately without making them sound better or worse than they are

When setting out to be truthful, consider the time and place that will make it most likely that the other person or persons will be able to really hear what you are saying.

You can live The Clover Practice™ of truth telling even in a society that does not particularly value honesty. You may already follow the path of rigorous honesty. If so, congratulations! You are well on your way to illness-proofing yourself. If you are committed to honesty, other people recognize it. "Living your truth inspires others and gives them permission to live their own true lives in a real, honest, and authentic way, too."[31]

Why Is the Truth So Scary?

Want to see a group of grown-ups get instantly nervous? Just say, "I am going to tell the truth and I want you to do the same." This will cause a noticeable response in most groups. People will go white or red in the face and start shuffling and coughing. Guaranteed that no one will say anything right away. In *Driving Fear out of the Workplace*, authors Kathleen Ryan and Dan Oestreich describe the results of interviews of 260 employees at all levels of the organization (manufacturing, service, and government) in various locations across the United States. Seventy percent of those they interviewed said they had hesitated to speak up at least once in the last few years for fear of repercussions. Loss of self-esteem was one of the negative impacts they reported for remaining silent. The authors concluded, "...The problem of fear is a widespread phenomenon, not isolated to a few workplaces."[32]

People fear getting fired, losing credibility, being perceived as a troublemaker, being passed over for promotions, being frozen out of resources. As a participant in one of my workshops said, "You can be punished in other ways besides getting fired. You can find yourself with no budget and not enough people." And this is true. But there is a name for that (punishing via withholding resources). It's called bullying, and you just have to ask yourself if you want to put up with it.

There is more than one dimension of honesty. There is the dimension of honesty about what is going on in our workplaces and there is the level of honesty about what is going on with us individually in our work. Hannegan says that most people build up a false shell so they can feel secure and safe. "We have built these shields to protect ourselves from knowing the truth and have allowed them to become the truth."[33] We believe our own press. We are terrified of admitting some things to ourselves, much less other people.

I have another thought on why the truth is so scary for most of us. I think that behind all our grown-up self-confidence, we are all still in high school. There is a fear in most of us that we are going to look bad and that someone is going to yell at us. No one wants to be the target of someone else's anger and disappointment and often our assumption is that we will be just that if we tell the truth.

Psychologists Robert Kegan and Lisa Laskow Lahey[34] talk about how our own "Big Assumptions" can create misery for us. They say that we unquestioningly believe "...that if we confront someone and he becomes terribly angry or terribly upset…well, it will simply be the end of the world. We do not hold our beliefs about conflict…as mere assumptions. We hold them as the truth…They are not so much the assumptions we have as they are the assumptions *that have us.* "[35]

Many of us assume that if the truth is known about how we are doing something, or something we forgot to do, or a mistake we made, terrible things *will certainly* happen. Sometimes, there are serious consequences to being forthright, but more frequently, it's our own assumptions and fears that "have us" and prevent us from speaking and acting with integrity.

The High Price of Fear

Hannegan points out that there's a high price to be paid for being controlled by fear. It depletes a person of emotional and physical energy.[36] Research supports the link between openness and immunity to illness too. So it's worth getting a handle on our own fears that someone is going to yell at us, or people won't like us if we are honest, or that we will lose our job or position.

If you are in an employment situation that requires you to lie or where the truth is badly distorted on a regular basis or where you can't speak up about what you see is happening, consider making a job change for the health of your spirit. Hannegan says that to leave a job and take a step into an unknown future can be terrifying. Many people, fearing loss and an unknown future, cling to jobs, relationships, and ways of life "even if it kills their souls."[37] Chapter 6 will help you think through your own situation.

Assessing the Risks

Following is a list of questions you can ask yourself if you are concerned about speaking up about an issue:

1. What has my experience been with this person before?
2. What is my motive for bringing this up?
3. What do I hope to get out of it?
4. Do I have enough information to support my observations?
5. What is the best I can hope for if I don't bring it up?
6. What is the worst thing that could happen if I do bring it up?
7. How realistic is my answer to #6?
8. Can I find a time and place to discuss this so the person can hear it?
9. Do I need to take someone else along?

How Am I Doing?

Table 1.3 includes opportunities to Tell the Truth, Always, in a work setting. After each statement place an X on the line indicating how easy or difficult it is for you. Nobody's perfect, so try to be accurate without being too hard on yourself. If the question doesn't fit your work situation, just skip it.

Table 1.3. How Easy or Hard Is It for Me?

1. Admit that I haven't finished/started a task that is due soon Easy for me_____Hard for me
2. Admit when I don't know how to do something and ask for help Easy for me_____Hard for me
3. Admit that I have information but that I am not at liberty to share it Easy for me_____Hard for me
4. Refuse to say that someone is "at a meeting" or "gone for the day" when he/she is not Easy for me_____Hard for me
5. Refuse to cover up information affecting the health and well-being of others Easy for me_____Hard for me
6. Refuse to repeat "misinformation" (something I know is not true) Easy for me_____Hard for me

7. State my honest reaction to an idea, proposal, or product, no matter whose it is

Easy for me_____Hard for me

8. Give a performance appraisal that is accurate based on what I have heard, seen, and experienced

Easy for me_____Hard for me

9. Refuse to distort information about other companies' or organizations' products or services to win business/good stuff for myself

Easy for me_____Hard for me

10. Admit when I have made a mistake and make any corrections that I can—sooner rather than later

Easy for me_____Hard for me

11. Choose the right time and place to tell my truth

Easy for me_____Hard for me

12. Describe problems/situations accurately without making them sound better or worse than they are

Easy for me_____Hard for me

Now look over your answers in Table 1.3. Respond to the next set of questions in Table 1.4 to figure out what it means and how you might make some changes.

Table 1.4. What It All Means

1. It is easier for me to Tell the Truth, Always, in situations where: _____
_____
_____

2. It is harder for me to Tell the Truth, Always, in situations where:
_____
_____

3. Look at the "harder for me" situations in question #2 above. What similarities do you see among those situations? Do you see any pattern (e.g., always involves a certain person, happens only with certain kinds of events or tasks, corresponds to how you are feeling physically, etc.)?
_____
_____

4. Select one situation you listed in question #2 in which you want to be able to Tell the Truth, Always. Write about what makes that situation an "honesty stumbling block" for you (e.g. fear of looking incompetent, being yelled at, losing compensation, don't want to hurt others' feelings, etc.).
_____
_____

5. How do you think this "honesty stumbling block" affects you (stress, worry, anger, guilt, fewer real relationships, etc.)?

_____

_____

6. On a scale of 1 to 10 where 1 is "Not Risky" and 10 is "Very Risky," how would you rate the risk of Telling the Truth, Always, in the situation(s) you described in Question 2? (Circle your answer.)

Not Risky   1 2 3 4 5 6 7 8 9 10   Very Risky

7. How realistic is your fear based on prior experiences with that person or group?

_____

_____

8. What is the worst that could happen to you if you Tell the Truth, Always, in that situation?

_____

_____

9. Write your goal—specifically what you intend to do, by when, why, and how you will know you are making progress in order to "Tell the Truth, Always."

_____

_____

_____

Reflection

If you have more X's on the "hard for me" ends of the lines in Table 1.3, consider this. Kaltman says that if lying seems the only practical response to a situation, there's a motive behind it. You are trying to solve a problem. Try brainstorming alternatives before giving up on telling the truth.[38] When we are stressed out, we can get tunnel vision and find it hard to see alternatives. Consciously slowing ourselves down and listing on paper what all the choices might be in a given situation can help us see alternatives to avoiding the truth.

Even when we wish to live a life of scrupulous honesty, we will still be telling the truth as we know it. We need to stay humble about our reality. "...Many a relationship has been damaged and a work setting poisoned because of *perfectly delivered* constructive feedback!"[39] So it matters *how* you speak your truth. In Chapter 2, Speak for Yourself, the second leaf of The Clover Practice™, provides ways to be truthful so others can hear what we are saying.

CHAPTER 2:
SPEAK FOR YOURSELF

There's only one corner of the universe you can be certain
of improving, and that's your own self.

— Aldous Huxley

In Longfellow's classic love triangle, *The Courtship of Miles Standish,* John Alden brings a marriage proposal to Puritan maiden Priscilla Mullins from his captain, Miles Standish. Her response was "Why don't you speak for yourself, John?" That was good advice.

Speak for Yourself, the second leaf of The Clover Practice™ showed itself as I struggled, as a management consultant, to speak truthfully to my clients. I knew that honesty was the basis for real relationships. "Strong relationships, careers, organizations, and communities all draw from the same source of power—the ability to talk openly about high-stakes, emotional, controversial issues."[40]

It is often said that people don't want to know the truth. I am not convinced of this. We may all be afraid of hearing certain truths. And we certainly don't want the truth brutally shoved in our faces. But imagine if you were walking down the hall with a toilet paper streamer trailing behind you. You would not enjoy hearing about it, but you would be glad to be informed. As we will see later in the chapter, it makes all the difference in the world how and when you tell your truth to another person.

What It Means

To Speak for Yourself means that you speak for the one and only person you are really entitled to speak for and that is your own self! Have you ever uttered or thought anything like this?

- I'm not sure how I feel about it.
- I don't know what to think about that.
- I don't know if I like it or not.
- I don't know how I would react if…

Chances are you have said these things, maybe even recently. They are honest statements of not knowing. So if we, who occupy our own minds and hearts, can be unsure of our own thoughts and feelings, how, then, can we be so sure about what other people are thinking and feeling?

In spite of this, most of us don't hesitate, especially if we are angry, to make statements to coworkers, bosses, even clients and customers that presume that we do know others' thoughts, motivations, and feelings.

If you listen to how people often talk to each other, you will find plenty of examples of people telling other people what they think. Here are some common ones:

- You don't care about this project.
- You don't understand.
- You only care about the dollars.
- You don't know what you are talking about.
- You are careless.
- You don't respect me.
- You did it on purpose.
- You always…
- You never…

The statements are all accusations of one kind or another, but they presume that the speaker knows what's in the head and heart of someone else. We never really do. We sometimes think we do.

To Speak for Yourself means that you approach any situation with an attitude of "This is what it looks like to me" instead of "You did (or did not do) this or that." It means starting with "I" and sticking with concrete language about what you saw, heard, and understood. It means avoiding language that sounds like you know another person's motives (e.g., "You don't care about the office."). It means being clear about what you want to happen.

Try Feedback Instead of Criticism

There is no such thing as constructive criticism. Criticism is criticism. It means finding fault. There is a place for criticism, for example, for concert pianists in training and Olympic athletes where the standard is perfection. But feedback will usually get you further in the workplace.

Feedback means sharing information on what did or did not happen in a situation. It does not involve a value judgment of good or bad, great or awful. Feedback involves:

- Facts as you see them (not opinions)
- What you saw happen (or not happen)
- Language that is specific and concrete (nonjudgmental)
- Description of the impact[41]

"You don't care about this project" might be said by Maria who feels that her project is not getting the support it should. It is a classic example of speaking as if we really know what's in someone else's head. It sounds like criticism and it won't get us very far with the other person.

In this scenario, a more effective alternative is for Maria to provide feedback by describing what she is seeing and how she is feeling. To speak for herself, Maria could say something like, "Looking at the budget we have for this project and the fact that I am now the only person working on it makes me think it's not a high priority. Am I reading this right?"

In posing this question, Maria lays out what she is noticing (the amount of dollars in the budget, the number of people working on it) and what conclusions she is drawing (it's a low priority). Then she checks for accuracy with the phrase, "Am I reading this right?" If she is told that the project is actually still a high priority, the door is open for her to request the resources she needs. If she is told that the project really isn't as high a priority as some others, she will have to decide how much time and energy she is willing to spend on it.

When you bring your own data (what you saw, heard, felt) to the table, you invite a much more authentic and useful response from the other person than accusing him or her of something. Conversely, if you routinely tell people what they are thinking, you engage their defenses and they will be so offended and/or worried about protecting themselves from you that they won't work on the issue you are discussing.

In our example, Maria's conversation *a la* Speaking for Yourself requires the other person to respond to her question and is a much stronger line of communication than, "You don't care about this project!"

The Help Desk Problem

Two people, Elliott and Hannah, staff a help desk. The Help Desk is available starting at 7:00 a.m. Monday-Friday. Hannah arrives every day before 7:00 a.m. and is taking calls at 7:00 a.m. as expected. Several times a week, Elliott arrives between 7:05 and 7:10 a.m., puts his lunch and jacket away, but isn't ready to work till almost 7:15. Hannah, who wants Elliott to be on the job when the phones start ringing, could say sarcastically, "You're always late. You must want to get fired."

Does Hannah's comment really solve the problem? Her sarcasm could make Elliott respond defensively. For one thing, he is not always late and it is not likely that he wants to get fired. If

Hannah is committed to speaking for herself, the conversation might go like this:

> I've noticed that this is the second time this week that you got here late. It's hard for me to be the only person here when the phones start ringing. I would appreciate it if you could start at seven o'clock every day too.

In this case, Hannah said what she had noticed, told him how it affects her, and asked him for a different behavior. It also leaves the door open for Elliott to say, "I've been staying later in the afternoon to make up the time, but I see what you mean." If the Speak for Yourself approach doesn't work, Hannah will probably have to ask a supervisor for help with the problem.

Pheng and the Project Switch

In another scenario, Pheng was moved off Project X, which had required weeks of building a relationship with a potential supplier. When told of being taken off the project and reassigned because he was needed more on Project Y, he might have said nothing and silently seethed. He might have shaken his head and told his boss, "You don't get it." But since he believed in the value of Speaking for Yourself, he said, "I'm very frustrated and angry (or any other colorful combination of words for "upset") that you took me off the project. I spent a lot of time with the supplier and I don't think it's a good idea to start with someone new. It feels like a step backward for me. I ask you to reconsider your decision and assign me back to the X

Project. I would be willing to help out on Project Y one day a week."

The sequence Pheng used is part of a traditional sequence of behavior modification from family therapy and one I used with students when I was a high school teacher. The steps are shown in Table 2.1.

Table 2.1. Traditional Behavior Modification Communication Sequence

1. When you _____
   (Describe the behavior.)

2. It makes me feel _____
   (Describe feelings.)

3. I would like you to _____
   (Describe hoped for actions and behaviors.)

4. I am willing to _____
   (Describe what you will do to improve the situation.)

5. Are you able/willing to do this (checking for agreement)?

This behavior modification model isn't bad. It is easy to use and it can help people focus on some key behavioral changes that need to be made. It is definitely better than accusations or violence or avoiding the problem altogether. The model does leave out, however, any opportunity for the other person or parties to talk about the situation from their points of view or propose other solutions.

Incidentally, The Clover Practice™ leaves room for people to be angry. Not everyone will be speaking calmly and quietly when something upsetting happens at work. The communication models discussed in this book will help you "Speak for Yourself." They give you a way to express your anger and disappointment so that others can hear it and hopefully make different choices next time around.

Everyone Has a Story about What Happened

In *Crucial Conversations,* authors Patterson, Grenny, McMillan, and Switzler prescribe a five-step dialogue process aimed at "creating a shared pool of meaning." The steps include:

1. Share your facts
2. Tell your story (what you think it all means)
3. Ask for others' paths
4. Talk tentatively
5. Encourage testing[42]

"Tell your story" is saying out loud what conclusions you are drawing from the facts. Especially in a high-stakes situation, these authors say, each of us takes the facts and creates our own story. ("He doesn't like me. She thinks I'm incompetent. He wants my job. She is taking it out on me," etc.) It might happen so quickly that we don't notice it. "Any set of facts can be used to tell an infinite number of stories."[43]

The authors urge us to be aware of the stories we tell ourselves in a conflict. "…Once they're told, the stories control us…We can tell different stories and break the loop. In fact, *until* we tell different stories, we *cannot* break the loop."[44]

Although the authors don't use the term "mental models," the stories we have in our heads about what is happening in any situation are based on our own mental models of how the world works. We need to acknowledge that we have these mental models that influence everything we see, hear, say, and do.

Remember the "Help Desk Problem" earlier in the chapter? Hannah could have told herself the story that Elliott was playing her for a sucker or "taking advantage" of her by not showing up on time. The real story could have been anything from Elliott is terribly disorganized to Elliott has a son with autism who is very difficult to get fed, dressed, and out of the house in the morning. Elliott still has to get to work on time, but because Hannah didn't presume any story, the door was open to finding a solution. (If Elliott really can't get to work at 7:00 a.m., even after he realizes the impacts, something has to change.)

Table 2.2 weaves the idea from *Crucial Conversations* that everyone has his or her own story of a given situation into a new and improved communication sequence. It is superior to the traditional behavior modification sequence shown in Table 2.1 because it provides more opportunities for back-and-forth communication.

Table 2.2. New and Improved Communication Sequence

1. When you _____
   (Describe the behavior.)

2. I interpret this as _____
   (Describe your "story.")

3. HOW DO YOU SEE THE SITUATION? (Provides a chance for others to tell their "story.")

4. I would like you to _____
   (Describe hoped for actions and behaviors.)

5. I am willing to _____
   (Describe what you will do to improve the situation.)

6. Are you willing to try it (checking for agreement)?

Using Tentative Language

"Speaking tentatively," as described by Patterson et al., is one way to acknowledge mental models. These authors recommend deliberately tentative statements such as

- In my opinion
- I'm beginning to wonder if...
- It's starting to look like[45]

Tentative statements like these are not wimpy.[46] They reflect humility and the willingness to admit that we might not have all the information. We have to say things in a way that other people can hear them. It does no good to use blaming or critical language. That just scares and alienates other people.

So in a conflict, if you Speak for Yourself, you are very clear about what you have seen and heard and what you think it means. You leave room for others to have their own views of what happened. Allowing more than one view of "the truth" will generally open up more alternatives for solving problems. (At the same time, you won't want to discount your views by saying something like, "I'm sure I don't know what I'm talking about.")

If you believe it's important to Speak for Yourself, you will

1. Speak directly to the person with whom you have a problem rather than talking to other people about it (avoiding triangulation).
2. Not tell anyone what anyone else said about him or her unless it is job- or life-threatening (telling tales).
3. Avoid gossip about other people's private lives.

For some people, these last two activities are some of the most interesting pastimes at work. But like quitting smoking, they are habits worth breaking.

Telling Tales

"Harold is really mad at you" is a typical example of telling tales—one person tells another about what someone else has supposedly said about him or her. You would think statements like this would be found only on playgrounds, but it is not uncommon to hear similar statements in any workplace.

Tattletale news is often a distortion of reality, having been filtered through the lens of at least one other (and maybe more) person. Maybe Harold is angry, but it may be at a situation and not an individual. Maybe Harold is angry, but it's about something no one even knows about. Bottom line—the message, as delivered, creates anxiety and fear and doesn't help anyone. Claiming that one person said something negative or derogatory about another is a common approach of psychopaths in the workplace, according to psychologists Paul Babiak and Robert Hare. "This 'divide and control' technique increases tension and distrust among individuals, effectively shutting down communication and providing cover for the psychopath. A psychopathic boss can use this technique to control and isolate employees from each other and to hide his or her abusive behavior."[47]

If you know that someone's work is being received less than favorably and the person is not likely to be made aware of it in any direct fashion, talk to that person out of earshot of other people. Suggest that he or she follow up with the appropriate individual(s). "I wanted you to know that there were questions about X at the meeting this morning. I think it would be good for you to follow up with Y to talk about it." That message sounds a lot different than "Ken didn't like your proposal."

Triangulation

Triangulation is the term used for talking to a third party about a problem one is having with someone else. Malicious triangulation involves intentionally saying negative things about that other party or casting that person in the worst possible light in order to strengthen one's own position. Sandelin says that this "…can occur very easily and spontaneously, you may not even realize what it has done until you analyze why you feel a certain way towards someone, or how you ever got such a wrong notion about someone. Malicious triangulation is very dysfunctional behavior and is one of the worst things that can happen in a community."[48]

I believe that a lot of triangulation is not malicious. Person A has a grievance against Person B, but complains to Person C. Even if there is no intent to cause harm, this approach is ultimately destructive to relationships. In the first place, Person B has no opportunity to make things right or do things differently. Person C now has unflattering information about Person B floating around in his or her head, but is not in a position to help the situation. In the meantime, Person A's problem remains unsolved.

Why doesn't Person A talk directly to Person B? It is usually out of fear, sometimes out of disrespect, sometimes out of laziness. The net effect of malicious and non-malicious triangulation can be much the same.

To Speak for Yourself means you will always talk to a person who has done something that has upset you or who is doing things that you don't want him or her to do.

Many of us are very uncomfortable with the idea of confronting another person. We may not have had a lot of positive models for problem solving in our families or the workplace. It might help to think of it differently. Instead of confronting another person, think of it as asking him or her to do things differently. There are surely situations where serious confrontation is essential as in cases of harassment or physical harm, but most work problems fall below this threshold.

If you Speak for Yourself, you will catch yourself whenever you start complaining about someone else at work, and take responsibility for talking directly to that person. You, yourself, may be convinced that nothing will be resolved by carping to a third party. But what if you are Person C and others are coming to you with complaints about coworkers? Even though they want to tell you, that doesn't mean you have to listen to it. Here are some things that you, as Person C, might say:

- Have you talked to him about it?
- When are you planning to talk to her about it? (This will shift the conversation in a different direction.)
- I would be willing to help you figure out the best way to talk to him or her about it.
- I wish [name] were here right now so you could work this out. I don't feel comfortable talking about [name] when he or she isn't here.

No-Gossip Zone

If you believe it is important to Tell the Truth, Always, and to Speak for Yourself, you cannot gossip about other people's private lives. Think about what gossip is—information about other people that is circulating, which may or may not be true. If you have played the old "telephone" game, you know how information gets distorted as it is told and retold. The fact that the boss got a promotion and will be leaving the office is not gossip—it's news. The rumor that the individual is having a secret affair with the new boss is gossip. You cannot repeat this if you are committed to truth and speaking from the one corner of the world you really know—your own.

> *How beautiful are the feet of those who bring good news,*
> *who proclaim peace, who bring good tidings...*
>
> Isaiah 25:7

Gossip wastes time, reduces productivity, and creates a low-trust work environment. Employee Assistance expert Robert Bacal says, "Gossip is destructive whether you are the target, or someone you don't like is the target."[49] He says that facing down gossip is an area where individuals can have a great deal of impact on their own. "In high-gossip workplaces, eventually, everyone will be the subject of gossip. Perhaps this week it's Fred, and next week it's Ann, but sooner or later, it IS going to get around to YOU."[50]

In the course of my workshops, I have asked people what they might say to stop a conversation that has taken a gossipy turn. Here is what they have suggested:

- I don't think we should talk about X when they aren't here to defend themselves.
- I don't think we have all the facts, so we really shouldn't be talking about it.
- It's really not our business.
- This doesn't seem right to me. How about those _____!! (Fill in the favorite team.)

If you are committed to The Clover Practice™, you will be able to walk away when the conversation gets ugly. When is it gossip versus just sharing news about what's happening in people's lives? Use the "invisible person" test to decide if it's gossip—would you be saying the same thing if the person were standing there?

What Are Your Motives?

Authors Kathleen Ryan, Dan Oestreich, and George Orr have written *The Courageous Messenger: How to Successfully Speak Up at Work.* The book offers step-by-step guidance on how to Tell the Truth, Always, from the time you first realize that you want to speak up about something to following up after you have had the conversation. They advise taking time to get clear on your motives for speaking up by asking yourself, "Why am I willing to bring this message forward?" Then ask, "And why is that important?" Then ask again why that reason is important. All told, repeat the why question five times. If you find yourself repeating the same answer, "you will know that you have found a core reason for speaking up."[51]

Choosing the Time to Speak for Yourself

As the first part of this chapter shows, it makes a difference *how* you say things to people. *When* you say things also matters. I know someone who confronted her supervisor in a packed room. There was nothing the supervisor could do about the situation at that moment. It looked like a deliberate attempt to humiliate. I don't think it was, but it had the same effect. The supervisor responded defensively and ultimately nothing was changed. Personally, I think the person with the complaint would have had a lot better luck discussing it either directly with the supervisor one-on-one or even in a smaller group.

Timing is everything. Hannegan suggests that when pent-up anger and frustration push us to the boiling point, this is not the time to finally speak the truth. She suggests giving yourself a "time out" first—a walk, a bike ride, a talk with a friend, even screaming at the top of your lungs.[52] "When you reach the point of volatility, you can no longer guarantee that you will remain in control of the situation and/or your own behavior. These situations are extremely dangerous in their potential repercussions to all involved. If at all possible, wait..."[53]

Bringing up an issue or complaint just before a big event or deadline isn't going to net the best results. Do you know when people you work with are best able to hear what you have to say? Some people are morning people and want to get things solved right off the bat. Some people can't be approached till after they have had their morning coffee.

What about you? If there's a problem, when and how do you hope people you work with will talk to you about it?

_____

_____

The "vehicle" or medium for your message also matters. I see more and more people in the workplace trying to solve conflict via e-mail. Don't do it! E-mail is great for many things, but solving problems between people is not one of them. Talk to the person face to face or at least pick up the phone. In addition to being a poor medium for solving conflict, e-mail should not be used for performance feedback or for sharing sensitive information about others. (Most people don't realize that their e-mail at work is the property of their employer and that it is not ever really confidential.)

Not a Free Ticket

A boss I had years ago attended a '70s-style sensitivity training workshop. Upon his return, he announced that he had learned that he could say anything he wanted to as long as he started with the words, "I feel." He continued his usual roughneck and bombastic treatment of employees, but dutifully started with "I feel" as in "I feel you are lazy and incompetent and on top of that, you are trying to kill me with that coffee you make." He had missed the point. "I feel" is a great start to a discussion, but you're supposed to stick to your own thoughts and feelings. It's not a free ticket to say anything you want about the other person's motives or attitudes.

Reflection

If we want to Tell the Truth, Always, so other people can hear it, our communication will have to be:

- Concrete and fact-based
- Grounded in our own understandings and observations
- Face-to-face
- Focused on getting good work done
- Focused on the current situation, not old history

Try it for the rest of this week. Listen to how people talk to each other. Pay attention whenever you hear anyone speaking for someone else by saying what someone else thinks or feels or believes. Listen for name-calling. Write the exact statements on a note card or on your calendar. Then look at the list. Do you see patterns? Have you said the same kinds of things? How useful are the comments? Do they help solve any problems? We really cannot know what is in the minds and hearts of other people. We might think we know, but this is not the same as knowing.

Speak for Yourself offers a way to Tell the Truth, Always, because you are speaking for the one person you are authorized to speak for—yourself. You are telling how you see a situation and leaving room for others to do the same. The philosopher Nietzsche says, "…If you wish to be a devotee of truth, then inquire."[54] If you wish to Speak for Yourself, you will find that you do at least as much asking as telling.

CHAPTER 3:
DECLARE YOUR
INTERDEPENDENCE

When we try to pick out anything by itself, we find it hitched to everything else in the universe.

— John Muir[55]

"Declare Your Interdependence" is the third leaf of The Clover Practice™. Recognizing how everything is connected can be a hard sell in a country that celebrates its *in*dependence every Fourth of July. Yet understanding our connections to each other and to the earth itself is our only hope for survival on the planet. For now, let's narrow it down to what interdependence means in the workplace.

We tend to think of workplaces as machines. If you doubt it, listen for machine metaphors at work. We talk about jump-starting something, putting on the brakes, putting wheels under a project, ramping something up or down. Does any other "machine" language come to mind for you? We think that if we take Action A we will get Result B, as if we were putting new spark plugs in an engine. We might not think that we will also get results Z and Q, which we never intended. Sometimes something as simple as changing a deadline for something has repercussions no one ever imagined. The machine metaphor is a simpleminded mechanistic view of the worlds we work in. International business leader, Arie de Geus, says, "I think every institution is a living system…these living systems are being threatened from the inside…[Employees] have no idea what they're doing there…and they have no idea how to create better conditions for the survival of the institution…On the contrary, they do all sorts of things that reduce the institution's life expectancy."[56]

It is difficult for us to see that our work organizations are more like living fabrics than machines. What happens in one part of the organization affects what happens in many other parts of the organization. It is difficult for us to see how what we do affects others in ways we would never dream of. It is difficult to see how our success is dependent on others succeeding. It is also difficult for us to see how we have a hand in creating our own problems.

The organizations we work in are organized according to principles of hierarchy that are created from human ideas of how things should be—God, king, president above and people below—but this view of reality as hierarchical is unnatural and artificial. "In nature, there is no 'above' or 'below,' and there are no hierarchies. There are only networks nesting within other networks."[57]

"Declare Your Interdependence" includes at least three dimensions, which, if we can really see them, can help us be more emotionally healthy at work.

1. No one succeeds in an organization by his or her own effort alone.

2. What happens in one part affects the whole.
3. When something is consistently going wrong in a work relationship, we are part of the problem.

The first of these means understanding how much our own fate is tied to that of our coworkers. The second means recognizing how every action can have repercussions far beyond what we intend. And the third is recognizing how big a role we may play in our own problems at work. We will take them one at a time.

No One Succeeds Alone

Our popular American heroes—the Lone Ranger, John Wayne, Rambo, Dirty Harry, the Terminator, Batman, Spiderman, Jason Bourne, Mr. and Mrs. Smith—are figures that act on their own and succeed on their own. None of these heroes is a team player. They are fictional characters for a good reason.

The truly rugged pioneer of the early American frontier has been recast today as the rugged individual who succeeds in the work world by brains, guts, and hard work, depending on no one else. It might be an appealing myth, but it is not very real. In the workplace, people do not succeed on their own. In the long run, as Robert Aitken puts it, "The fundamental fact is that I cannot survive unless you do."[58]

Each of us is part of a system of other people, a fact that is overwhelmingly obscured by our mythology. Ask anyone on the street, "Who saved Chrysler in the 1970s?" and they will probably say Lee Iacocca. We want to believe in the Lone Ranger. But

Doug Fraser, a professor at Wayne State University and former president of United Auto Workers, has said, "Much is written about Lee Iacocca. It's the Chrysler workers who saved Chrysler Corp."[59]

That we are interdependent at work was a lesson I learned from Andy the dishwasher. During college, I worked as a server in a fancy hotel with an even fancier dining room. Guests at this dining room were treated to meals cooked right at their tables. My job was to make fresh Caesar salads and cook flaming Steak Diane, Bananas Foster, Cherries Jubilee, and other lusciously dramatic dishes.

Andy (not his real name) was a developmentally disabled adult from a nearby institution whose job was to wash dishes for this dining room. He was gung ho about his dishwashing job, showed up in freshly laundered whites every day, on time. To anyone's memory, Andy had never missed a shift in the years he had been there. He would stop you in the kitchen and ask how things were going, "Were the dishes as clean as you wanted? Are you happy with my work?" People secretly made fun of him for caring so much about his humble job of dishwashing.

One Saturday night, Andy didn't show up for work. No one had even noticed till the dishes started piling up. I hope I can adequately describe the disaster. Those of us who were servers on this busy night were washing dishes for our tables. I still remember looking through trays of dirty dishes to find particular dishes and utensils to wash! Naturally, our dishwashing meant less time to take care of our very discriminating customers. People waited for their food while we hunted for clean soup bowls. The shrimp cocktails edged from crispness to limpness while we scoured dirty trays for cocktail forks to wash. I left exhausted, undertipped because our service hadn't been up to par, and dismayed at the pile of dishes that still remained. I never knew who cleaned up that mountain of dishes, but I know that the next time I saw Andy at his post with the sprayer, I was grateful. I realized in a very concrete way that the dishwasher and I needed each other to be successful.

Years later, I worked with a manufacturing company in a consulting role. Again it was brought home to me how little we understand our mutual dependence as workers in the same organization. It all started with an enormous Wisconsin-style potluck of cheese and crackers and cut-up veggies, sausage, chips and dip, and cake. It took two tables to hold all the goodies.

I came upon the treats while interviewing workers in a factory. The office workers who cheerfully ushered me in to the conference room explained that the spread of food was in honor of an office birthday. I, a stranger, was urged to have as much of the food as I could eat, as there was "so much."

One man after another came off the factory floor to be interviewed by me. Their faces were covered with a fine powder from their machines. They were sweaty and wore old clothes. Each one commented on how nice it was to be cool in the air-conditioning. Each one answered my questions forthrightly.

One man in particular eyed the food with apparent longing. I invited him to take a plate because there was "so much." He picked up a six-inch paper plate and put on it a few slices of cheese and some crackers and chips. While he was filling his plate, I went back into the office, which was separated from the conference room by a glass window. Three office workers, nicely dressed in nylons and pumps, stood at the window with arms folded and faces screwed up in distaste. "Look! Someone from the *plaanntt* is taking food," one said. The other two "hmmphed" their disdain.

Their tone suggested that these office workers felt superior to that tired and dusty factory worker. When I told them that I had invited him to take a plate, they looked at me as if I were a traitor. His labor made it possible for them to have their jobs and to work in a cool and comfortable office. It seemed that they had no sense of their debt to him and to the other plant workers.

I've been upset about this incident ever since. And I have seen the same kind of thinking in a variety of other organizations. A woman in Australia, commenting on The Clover Practice™, told me that she had worked for the government distributing various payments to families, students, those who were disabled, or on welfare, unemployed, etc. She said, "The overwhelming idea amongst the workers was that 'we' were somehow above 'them,' even though, strictly speaking, if these people didn't have problems, or if the government decided to pay the tax breaks by a different method, we wouldn't have a job. In short we depended on our clients."

Many people cannot acknowledge that no matter how talented or deserving they are, they need the other people in the organization in order to succeed. The connections may be hard to see. The most skilled surgeon in the world will not be successful if the people who sterilize the instruments, process the blood tests, and clean up after the last surgery do their jobs poorly. At the moment when they are doing their jobs, the people who answer the phones, figure out the payroll, keep the electricity and heat on, plow the lots, keep the computer network running, and wash the dishes (to name a few) are just as essential as the more visible "stars" of the organization.

And not only do we need our coworkers, we need our customers and clients as well. Incidentally, we need the stars too—we need everyone to have a successful enterprise whether it's a surgical suite or a concrete-pouring operation.

We Americans don't like to think about our interdependence. As Meg Wheatley describes it, "We have raised individualism to its highest expression, each of us protecting our boundaries, asserting our rights..."[60] But to think that we succeed in an organization on our own merit and effort alone is mostly a delusion. I wonder what we would do differently if we really appreciated the fact that our success depends on other people doing their work well. In Table 3.1, you are invited to think about the people or groups who make it possible for you to be successful on the job.

Table 3.1. Who Contributes to My Success at Work?

1. Whom do you depend on to be successful in your work (people or groups)?

_____

_____

2. What might you do differently to make sure that the person or group in question #1 is successful? (Examples might be sharing information more often or willingly or widely, expressing appreciation, including people in events, meetings, etc.)

_____

_____

_____

_____

What Happens in One Part Affects the Whole

We have inherited organizations that seem purposely designed to make it hard to see outside of our own cubes. We are organized by function—marketing separated from production separated from customer service. We have rules about what level can talk to another level. We think the organizational chart depicts reality. Competitions are purposely staged between sales leaders or units with monetary rewards attached. Some leaders think that people don't notice or don't care how others are treated. "All living beings are members of ecological communities bound together in a network of interdependencies. When this deep ecological perception becomes part of our daily awareness, a radically new system of ethics emerges."[61]

In one organization, an individual was promoted to an executive position that she had neither the experience nor the skills to handle. She was a good person who had helped a top executive for many years. To show his appreciation, he had promoted her. It didn't take long for her lack of preparation for the job to become evident. Within a year, she was removed from the position against her will. She was placed in a lower position within the organization. Her vociferous complaints and problems adjusting caused her to be assigned to an outbuilding away from the main office. She was the only staff member assigned to that building, although she came in for breaks and lunch. When she came into the cafeteria, everyone noticed her. People commented on "poor Jean" (not her real name) and fewer and fewer people wanted to interact with her. Do you think Jean's situation affected other people? Of course it did. Those responsible for the decision, however, remained unaware of how what had happened to Jean was affecting the morale of the entire organization. Everyone knew deep down, "It could happen to me."

We Are Competing with the Wrong People!

In an organization I know of, long ago before computers were the norm, a top-level administrator went into another administrator's office after work hours and took the final copy of a grant proposal that was due the following day. The reason? The top-level person wanted the proposal to come from his unit within the organization. The one who had been burglarized was beside himself when the final proposal could not be found. He knew he had left it on his desk after reviewing it at the end of the day. When the grant was awarded to the top-level administrator, it was clear what had happened. You can imagine the bad feelings that surrounded that grant, not to mention the time and effort that had been wasted in developing the proposal that ended up in the dumpster. In a different scenario, the two units could have worked together on a proposal, but competition was the prevailing "ethic" within that organization.

> ...*you can't hurt another person without hurting your-*
> *self, nor can you help another person without helping*
> *yourself.*
>
> – Wayne W. Dyer[62]

I often wish I could take all the energy that organizations expend on competing internally and refocus it on serving customers and stakeholders better and competing with the real competitors. Unfortunately, our organizations are designed and managed to stoke internal competition. It doesn't have to be that way. For example, in Japan, industrial espionage is fierce. The plans and equipment for spying on competitors are worthy of James Bond. Yet, within any given Japanese company, the watchword is cooperation. People routinely work in different parts of the organization to better understand the enterprise as a whole. (This is done in both business and government.) All parts of the organization are focused together on creating a successful product or service. The Japanese approach is not what most of us have. You cannot change the prevailing values of the organization you work in. You can step back, however, and ask yourself the questions in Table 3.2 aimed at uncovering your connections to others in your organization.

Table 3.2. My Work: Where It Comes from and Where It Goes

1. Who provides me with what I need to do my work? (That is, who makes sure that you have the information or leads or customers or patients or students or drills to do your work?)

   _____

2. What can I do to make sure that person or group continues to provide me with what I need when I need it? What kinds of information, follow-up, communication, appreciation, etc. can I provide?

   _____

   _____

   _____

3. Whom do I hand off my work to? Who receives the results of my work? (For example, if you are a nurse, it is the patients, families, and possibly other health care providers. If you are a metal fabricator, it may be the final customer or another person or production group. If you are a teacher, it is other educational levels and/or employers. If you are in sales, you may hand off to production.)

   _____

4. What can I do to make sure I hand off my completed work when and how it is needed? (This will probably require asking some questions of those who are in the next stage of whatever work process you are part of.)

   _____

   _____

By answering the questions in Table 3.2 about how you can be most effective in the work you personally do, right where you are today, you can avoid some of the stress and conflict that inevitably arises because our organizations are designed more to pit people against one another rather than to cooperate.

Thinking about Unintended Consequences

Because of our dim sense of how interdependent we really are in our workplaces, it is easy to underestimate how much our work and the everyday decisions we make affect other people. If you are in a leadership role, you are making decisions every day that affect the whole organization. If you are not in a formal leadership position, you may think that you don't make decisions that affect other people. But everyone does—the choice of which task to tackle, which meeting to go to, whom we allow to get appointments, whose work will get priority, whether to shorten or extend a deadline, what changes to make on forms or applications—these are all like rocks thrown in a pond that create larger and larger circles. The circles can be good or not such good outcomes or a mixed bag, but every decision we make at work will have impacts beyond ourselves.

Death by Operating System

I recall working on a deadline for a book manuscript. Every minute counted if I was going to be able to make the deadline. (Never mind how I happened to be up against the deadline. I am sure it was my own fault, but that's where I was.) I came to work one morning after working late on the book the night before and found that a new operating system had been installed on my computer overnight. The screen was unrecognizable to me. I remember the stomach-lurching calls to find out what had happened. I couldn't even find my manuscript, much less work on it. An information technology worker had been told to install the system in the night so as not to disrupt the workday. This person never thought that I would be panicked by the new icons and procedures. He had no idea of how his actions would affect my work. To help me, the technician reinstalled the old system and then reinstalled the new system after I was done with the book, but it meant double work for him and extra gray hair for me.

I am always amazed at how casually people will look at data that is created by a system or process and say, "We don't need that. Let's not collect it anymore." They do so without ever stopping to think that the data is used by other people or offices and they need it to do their work.

What can we do about the fact that our actions can have an impact far beyond what we ever intended? We can only ask these kinds of questions every day:

- How is this going to affect other people and other parts of the organization?
- Whom do I need to talk to before I make the change I am considering?
- What are some possible unintended consequences of what I am doing? What could I do now to avoid them?

And how does this help you stay emotionally healthy? When you acknowledge and honor the connections, the amount of conflict and problems with other people or other offices will decrease. You will have more time to spend doing your work rather than putting out fires. You will have less stress and thus better health. Less stress, better health, more peace of mind.

Many years ago, a very wise friend and mentor said, "Whenever you solve a problem, the best you can hope for is that the problem you solved is bigger than the one you just created." I used to think that was pessimistic, but now I know that he understood how interconnected things are. He was right.

We Contribute to Our Own Problems

If a problem has persisted for any length of time between us and another person or group, we are contributing to the problem. This last part of "Declare Your Interdependence" is probably the least fun. We don't want to think that we are part of our own problems, but we inevitably are. We may not be contributing 50-50 to the trouble. We may be responsible for only 10 percent of it, but we are part of it. It takes an enormous amount of maturity to see this and to act on it.

I have noticed that some workplaces have long histories and reputations of being bad places to work. Even when the staff has completely or almost completely turned over, the backbiting, uncooperative, deceitful, nasty, frightening, bullying (choose as many as apply) culture continues. It's almost as if the dysfunctional practices have soaked into the bones of the organization and are repeated over the years by some kind of unconscious agreement of the employees. One woman who worked in a department like that said, "I've been here for twenty years and it's been the same since the day I started—people are treated like dirt." How is this woman contributing to the problem? I hope you said she is staying in a workplace that does not value her or anyone else. She could vote with her feet, but she has chosen not to.

> *To put the world right in order, we must first put the nation in order; to put the nation in order, we must first put the family in order; to put the family in order, we must first cultivate our personal life; we must first set our hearts right.*
>
> – Confucius

Layne and Paul Cutright, authors of *You're Never Upset for the Reason You Think,* say each of us must take "radical personal responsibility" for what happens to us. They say, "We call it radical because it is such a departure from what is commonly thought of as responsibility, which can mean laying blame. Instead, it is insight into the deeper workings of your mind that illuminates how you have contributed to any challenging situation before you."[63]

In Chapter 4, you will have a chance to think about how much of how you see the world and behave every day was programmed into you by your family and life experiences. Right now you have the opportunity to make different choices about your own actions and how you will respond to things that happen at work. Recognizing family patterns might help you see how your actions trigger or extend certain kinds of problems. Being more aware of how we interpret situations through our own personal lenses can help us make different choices about how we will handle these situations.

How Can I Recognize My Part in My Problems?

Besides doing your emotional homework, as discussed in Chapter 4, you can ask yourself several questions when there is a problem at work between you and another person or group or between your work group and others:

1. Am I doing things that will make this conflict get worse (e.g., excluding people who would ordinarily be involved in an activity, cutting off communication, doing things intentionally to irritate)?
2. If I were "the other side," how would my/our actions look?
3. Have I experienced this kind of trouble before? Is there possibly a pattern that I am unconsciously reliving?
4. Have I spoken directly with the people involved (Chapter 2) or have I made an effort to directly address this problem in some way?
5. What can I do to get things back on track so we can focus on the work we have to do?

The important thing to realize is that you have a choice in how you respond to the problems and conflicts that are a part of every workplace on earth. You won't be able to avoid problems, but you can be fully conscious about your role in them.

Reflection

"…There is a cloud floating in this sheet of paper. Without a cloud, there will be no rain: without rain, the trees cannot grow; and without trees we cannot make paper. The cloud is essential for the paper to exist."[64] This is how author Thich Nhat Hanh begins his discussion of the interconnectedness of all things. He says that if we look into the piece of paper we will see the sunshine that made the forest grow, and the logger and his parents, and the wheat for their bread, and everything else that contributed to growth of the trees. He says we can even see ourselves because the paper is part of our perception. He concludes, "As thin as this sheet of paper is, it contains everything in the universe in it."[65] In living The Clover Practice™, we recognize our interconnections. We "Declare our Interdependence" and in doing so, navigate the work world with increased awareness, skill, and confidence.

CHAPTER 4:
DOING YOUR EMOTIONAL HOMEWORK

But the big things—how we think, what we value—those you must choose yourself.

– Morrie Schwartz
from *Tuesdays with Morrie*[66]

There is no way around it. Every grown-up who wants to be emotionally healthy and at peace needs to so do some psychological homework. Doing this work is a way to "Tell the Truth, Always" to ourselves.

What Homework?

Growing up, by its nature, is a wounding process. At best, in growing up we suffer loss of childhood's dreams and the times when someone else took care of us. At worst in growing up, we suffer the loss of people we love or, in our vulnerable state, neglect, cruelty, or molestation. No matter what the family situation was—great or terrible—every grown-up needs to do some emotional homework.

A whole range of growing-up experiences can affect your success on the job and your satisfaction with your work. Some families are overcautious and raise children who become frightened of change or doing new things as adults. Some families—a lot of families actually—are so afraid of conflict that no one ever says anything about problems or anger. These families can produce a legacy of anger that boils just under the surface and that is passed from one generation to another and that also shows up in the workplace.

A man describes his family when he was growing up as what "…looked like the perfect family from the outside—tidy, well-mannered, regular church-goers." But the family rule was that only the parents were permitted to show anger. The children were not allowed to express anger or disappointment or dis-agreement for fear of the belt buckle. He says, "I grew up feel-ing like I didn't have a mouth. I just had to take it." This man is Hollywood-handsome, intelligent, and college educated, but suffers from debilitating self-doubt. He works long hours but takes little satisfaction from his work. He longs for retirement, which is years away. He has a hard time speaking for himself at work and finds himself feeling like he did as a child. He has recognized the similarity between his childhood feelings and his feelings in his current work situation. He has begun doing his emotional homework.

Some families hold beliefs that are paralyzing to children who grow into adults. Rigid ideas about what girls should do and what boys should do persist into adulthood and can prevent people from using their talents or achieving success.

Some families believe it is better to lie and look good than to Tell the Truth, Always, and admit to being flawed. This can affect adults' abilities to admit when they have made mistakes (making it hard to fix them) in the workplace, or to admit when they don't know how to do something, or to say that they don't understand what they are supposed to be doing, or to admit when they cannot reasonably handle their workload.

Some wounds from childhood are imposed by peers. Kira (not her real name), a beautiful and talented twenty-one-year-old woman recalls a friend from grade school and middle school who "held her hostage" emotionally by threatening to kill herself if she did not do exactly what her friend dictated. The friend did actually attempt suicide once and it was Kira who alerted the girl's mother. Strangely enough, this painful and frightening relationship was primarily carried on through telephone calls and Internet chats, so the situation was invisible to the parents of either girl. Kira says now, "When it was going on, I didn't know what to do. I thought I just had to take it. Now I know that I will never let myself be so controlled like that by another person."

As a consultant who has worked in many organizations and talked to many people about their work, it is not difficult for me to think of people who are in work situations that sound very much like Kira's adolescent friendship that was based on fear and control.

One man was haunted into middle age by an instance of childhood sexual abuse inflicted by a stranger. The pedophile had lured the little boy with promises to show him toys. His parents never knew of the molestation. The shame had stayed with him for decades, affecting everything he did and every relationship he was in. He was fired from his first professional job for under-performing in spite of the fact that he was very intelligent and good looking. It was not until the man was in deep therapy that he was able to say what had happened to him and could begin healing and living his life more successfully.

Some people who have extraordinarily painful childhood experiences grow up to be successful adults in their work and personal relationships. Researchers estimate that about 15 percent of those who make it through the most abusive or fearful experiences growing up ultimately become high-functioning adults.[67] Even individuals who survived terrible experiences and still ended up with positive self-images may find themselves using coping mechanisms from childhood that don't serve them well as adults. One common example is excessively "taking care" of other people to the point where it hurts their own health and well-being.

The other 85 percent whose wounding in early life is still keeping them from being successful can discover their inner strength and gain confidence, but only by purposely working toward this goal. Marsha Sinetar, author of *Do What You Love, The Money Will Follow: Discovering Your Right Livelihood,* says there are usually two ways to do this. The first is becoming more aware of what happened to them (which you are doing right now). She says, "The second and perhaps the more important way is by dealing with the very things they find most difficult. At some point, they must face their own difficulties related to goals they may have long ago discarded as impossible…"[68] They have to do their grown-up emotional homework. We all do.

The philosopher Schopenhauer says, "...The experiences and illuminations of childhood and early youth become...the categories according to which all later things are classified—not always consciously, however. And so it is that in our childhood years the foundation is laid of our later view of the world...it will be in later years unfolded and fulfilled, not essentially changed."[69] I am much more optimistic than Schopenhauer. I believe that by stepping back and reflecting on our life experiences, we can make some independent choices. As an adult, each of us has, in fact, an obligation to figure out our own values, choose our own behaviors, and be aware of family problems that we may have inherited.

Inherited Values and Beliefs

Most of our values—what we think is important in life or how we think we should act—were learned unconsciously as we grew up. "The process of absorbing them was invisible to you, so you didn't notice you were doing it. It happened silently, in the background of your life. The process of absorbing your beliefs was invisible to you...Regaining that awareness and accepting personal responsibility is an acquired skill."[70]

What was most valued in your family? Religion? Education? Money? Careers? Relationships? Travel? Looking good? Physical fitness? Having fun? Sports? Food? Cleanliness? Entertaining? Generally time, effort, and money are focused in the areas that the family values. Values and beliefs are mostly inherited, but new values can be introduced into a family by a change of location, job, or living situation.

Some values and beliefs are inherited backward. For example, adults may be scrupulously punctual because members of their families were chronically late when they were growing up. Even though it's the opposite value, it's still inherited.

Think about what was really valued in the family in which you grew up and the strongly held beliefs. Write your answers in Table 4.1. Pay more attention to what your family actually did and where they focused their attention than to what they said. Talk is cheap.

Table 4.1. Family Beliefs and Values

As I think about where my family put effort, focus, and dollars when I was growing up, I think that we believed in and/or valued these things very highly:

There are no right or wrong answers to this next question. But look at each value or belief you listed in Table 4.1 and ask yourself three questions:

1. Is this something I value and hold dear myself?
2. Is this where I want to put my focus, effort, and dollars?
3. Is this what I want my children (or the children in my life) to value as well?

Now circle the family beliefs and values (Table 4.1) that you can truly say you hold dear yourself, want to live out, and want to pass on to future generations. Are there any leftovers? Are there values or beliefs from your family that you don't accept or don't embrace to nearly the same degree of intensity? If so, give yourself permission to let go of the values that were passed down to you, but that don't work for you. In Table 4.2 you can list and think more about those "leftover" values.

Table 4.2. Leftover Values

1. Even though my family valued: _____   _____   I am making a different choice in my life. Instead, I value: _____   _____
2. Have any of the "leftover" values impacted my work and career? If so, how?   _____   _____
3. How would a new belief and value make me more successful in my work life?   _____   _____
4. What values/beliefs are missing? What do I value or believe that my family did not necessarily hold to be very important?   _____   _____

You and I have, not only the privilege, but the obligation to ourselves and our own families of stepping back from the values and beliefs that were handed down to us and making a conscious decision about whether to hold them close or let them go. If you do not do this work, you are living out the script of someone else's play.

If you are very clear in your own mind about what's important to you, it will help you make many work-related decisions, including possibly the most difficult career decision of all—whether to leave or stay in a particular job.

Inherited Practices and Behaviors

Practices and behaviors, like values, beliefs, and quilts, are handed down in families. By practices, I mean how we usually do things. Practices and behaviors are based on values and are, in fact, the values in action. Here are some typical family practices:

- We never yell at each other. We just don't talk if we are mad.
- We have food for happy times and celebrations.
- We have food when something sad has happened.
- We always have a big dinner on Sunday after church.
- We always take a vacation together as a family in August.
- We plant a tree every Father's Day.
- We never go to bed with dirty dishes in the sink.
- We always keep the bathroom door closed at all times.
- We never turn on the air conditioner if the outside temperature is below 81 degrees.

- We scream at each other if we are mad, but we make up soon after.
- We respect other people's privacy to the max.
- We don't worry about people's privacy. We don't have anything to hide.
- At the holidays, we always save the bows and paper for next year.
- We always go someplace warm for spring break.
- Parents always go in to work in the evenings and weekends.
- Parents always work third shift.
- We tell "white lies" to spare the feelings of others.
- We say whatever is on our mind at any given time.
- Everyone gets married and has children.
- We cry when we get emotional.
- We never cry.

You can see that the family practices vary widely in their impact and importance. Whether or not you wash all the dishes before you allow yourself to go to bed at night is much less important than how you deal with anger. But these practices are usually deeply ingrained in us. One of the big challenges of marriage, for example, is figuring out what family practices a couple will observe, given that each individual comes to the marriage with a long history of "doing things" in a certain way.

As with values, we have the privilege and responsibility to figure out if the practices we inherited from our birth families are the ones we want for our own lives.

It takes a certain amount of emotional work to step back from our "preprogrammed" life practices and behaviors and decide for ourselves if we want to keep them. It is a process that you probably won't be able to do at one sitting. Many of the values and behaviors are such a part of your life that you may not even be aware of them. List at least three family practices/behaviors in Table 4.3. Do they work for you? Do you want to replace the practice that was handed down to you with a new practice? What would it be?

For example, one woman said that she wanted to change a family practice of blaming someone in the family when something went wrong. "Somebody's head had to roll," she said, "if something got broken or plans got ruined." She wrote in the second column, "When something goes wrong, I want us to figure out together how to prevent it from happening next time."

Table 4.3. Inherited Practices or Behaviors vs. What I Want for My Life

Practices or Behaviors from the Family I Grew up in That I Would Like to Change:	The Practices or Behaviors I Want for My Life:

The values and beliefs, practices, and behaviors you inherited from your family will greatly influence the kind of work you choose, the way you behave at work, how much negativity in the workplace you are willing to deal with, how important it is for you to progress in your career, how you see your role at work, and the like. That is why it is important that you yourself do to the work of choosing the practices and values for your own life rather than blindly accepting what you have been handed. As we make these conscious choices about what we want for our lives, it takes us up a couple of notches on the way to being a grown-up.

Inherited Problems, Patterns, and Addictions

You might be feeling protective toward your parents or cherished memories of childhood. This is fine. Many people did not experience parents who were emotionally healthy themselves. Your inclination may be to say, "Just get over it!" I am all for getting over it, but you have to recognize it before you can get over it. And once you recognize your wounds, you must take action to heal.

Some people grew up in families that had serious problems. These problems led the children to behave in a certain way, for example being hypersensitive to others' moods or caretaking or people pleasing. Even as adults, we will naturally tend to hang on to the behaviors that worked when we were children in troubled situations. These behaviors are often below our level of consciousness. We don't even know we are doing them.

Unless we recognize those old patterns, we will replay in our jobs scenarios from the families in which we grew up. Children who grow up in families where the adults were impaired by chemicals are always affected by the experience. Adult children of addicts as a group share some common characteristics such as low self-esteem and difficulty with relationships. There are many great books on this topic and I've listed a few at the end of the chapter. If you are the adult child of an alcoholic or drug addict it will affect you every minute of every day on the job unless you do your emotional work.

Many kinds of addiction have nothing to do with substances. Dr. Aviel Goodman, director of the Minnesota Institute of Psychiatry, offers a definition of addiction that goes beyond chemicals. Goodman says that an addiction is a process in which

> a behavior, that can function both to produce plea-
> sure and to provide escape from internal discom-
> fort, is employed in a pattern characterized by
>> (1) recurrent failure to control the behaviour
>>   (powerlessness) and
>> (2) continuation of the behaviour despite sig-
>>   nificant negative consequences (unmanage-
>>   ability).[71]

You can be addicted to other people, food, worrying, sex, cybersex, work, the Internet, collecting junk, shopping, exercise, etc. People can even be addicted to perfection. (Angeles Arrien says, "When we are addicted to perfection, we begin to walk the procession of the living dead."[72]) What all addictions have in common is that they reduce one's choices and cause harm to ourselves or others. Experts estimate that 40 percent of the population will have an addiction problem at some point in their lives.[73]

Over time, addictions erode people's basic common sense, compassion, and consideration. Plus, they require a lot of energy to maintain. A man who is addicted to perfection will never be able to relax, as he will be working constantly to make things perfect. A woman with a relationship addiction will have little time or energy to devote to anything except "the relationship." All these active addictions will play themselves out at work in one way or another.

If you have an untreated addiction to anything right now, it will be difficult to act according to The Clover Practice™. You will find it very difficult to "Tell the Truth, Always." You will be more likely to focus on what other people are doing or not doing, so you won't be likely to "Speak for Yourself." And you may not be able to see at all how you are contributing to your own problems, as your judgment may be too impaired to "Declare Your Interdependence." This is an ideal time to get professional help.

Because you are reading this book, you are willing to work on improving your own life. Chances are that you have developed life skills and abilities that can lead to work satisfaction. As your next step, complete the questions in Table 4.4 "When I was Growing Up: What Happened to Me."

The statements in the left-hand column describe childhood experiences that are damaging or potentially damaging. These experiences can result in "old movies playing" below your level of awareness that can hold you back or make your work life miserable. Answering the questions will give you an idea of areas that may be problematic to you as an adult.

Table 4.4. When I Was Growing Up: What Happened to Me

When I was growing up:	Yes	No	Don't Know
1. I was expected to be perfect.			
2. My parents seemed too busy to pay attention to me.			
3. I was spanked to the point of bruises or bleeding.			
4. We had a rigid family schedule that we could not deviate from.			
5. I was not allowed to express anger or disagreement.			
6. I was responsible for caring for other family members so that it interfered with school or friendships.			
7. Lying was common in my family.			
8. I saw family members being hit or verbally abused even though I was not.			
9. Our family kept secrets.			

When I was growing up:	Yes	No	Don't Know
10. One or more family members were impaired by alcohol or drugs daily or weekly.			
11. I was hit by a family member.			
12. I tried to protect others from being hit or verbally abused.			
13. I was sexually abused.			
14. One or both of my parents had secret extramarital affairs.			
15. One or both of my parents were ill for a long time.			
16. One or both of my parents died.			
17. We did not have enough food or clothing or housing to be physically comfortable.			
18. There was constant anger and bitterness between my parents.			
19. I felt like I was a spouse to my parent rather than a kid.			
20. Family religious practices made it difficult to participate in school or with friends.			
21. A particular activity dominated my parents' lives so that they didn't pay attention to me (cleaning, shopping, TV, gambling, eating, etc.).			
22. I was afraid of my father.			

When I was growing up:	Yes	No	Don't Know
23. I was afraid of my mother.			
24. My parents were fearful of many things.			
25. I was constantly worried that we wouldn't have enough money to get by.			
26. I was afraid that one or both of my parents would leave.			
27. My family believed that women should **never** work outside the home.			
28. My family believed that men should **always** be the sole financial support for their families.			
29. One or more of my parents or grandparents were addicted to alcohol or drugs.			
30. My parents or other family members fought a lot.			
31. Conflicts were never handled openly. Problems were shoved under the rug.			
32. People teased me about how I looked or other imperfections.			

Impacts of Childhood Problems on Adult Work Life

This is a book about waking up—becoming aware of our own pasts, our behavior now, and the futures we can have.

Robert Aitken describes what can happen when we take time to become aware: "...When your boss or somebody else takes up a role in the old family play that formed your life, you can say, 'Oh, I remember you' and the pain will be reduced."[74]

In Table 4.5, childhood experiences are paired up with workplace behaviors that may result. The behaviors are common responses to childhood traumas, not absolute predictions. Many of these behaviors were coping mechanisms developed when we were children, but they have actually become a liability to us as working adults. The reality is that childhood wounds can lead to any of the workplace behaviors in the right-hand column.

You will notice that some of the behaviors shaped by childhood wounds can be totally opposite. People can go to extremes, for example, either over performing or underperforming. Feel free to add behaviors under "Other" that you are aware of in yourself that may have carried over from your past experiences.

Look at the items where you checked yes in Table 4.4, "When I was Growing Up." Circle the number of those items in Table 4.5 "Behaviors Now."

Table 4.5. Behaviors Now

When I Was Growing Up:	Behaviors Now
1. I was expected to be perfect.	1. Has expectations of others that are unrealistic or unattainable because self-expectations are so high. 2. Overworks to the point of exhaustion regularly. 3. Cannot admit to mistakes. 4. Will not ask for help even if job is in jeopardy. 5. Is careless and sloppy in work habits. 6. Other: _____
2. My parents seemed too busy to pay attention to me.	1. Takes credit for work of others. 2. Lets others take credit for his/her work. 3. Dominates every meeting. 4. Seeks attention through inappropriate clothing or behavior. 5. Works below level of skills or talents. 6. Other:_____
3. I was spanked to the point of bruises or bleeding.	1. Overly harsh verbally toward coworkers or direct reports. 2. Believes he/she is not worthy of an appropriate salary or working conditions. 3. Stays stuck in a poor job situation. 4. Fumes silently rather than speaking up. 5. Other:_____
4. We had a rigid family schedule that we could not deviate from.	1. Has difficulty changing plans. 2. Not able to be flexible when required. 3. Overly critical of coworkers and direct reports. 4. Extremely uncomfortable with change or ambiguity. 5. Regularly late for appointments. 6. Other:_____

When I Was Growing Up:	Behaviors Now
5. I was not allowed to express anger or disagreement.	1. Does not speak up when workload is overwhelming or when conditions are unreasonable. 2. Fearful of anger in others. 3. Exhibits anger often and inappropriately at work. 4. Verbally abuses others. 5. Frequently gets locked into conflict with others. 6. Fumes silently rather than speaking up. 7. Other:_____
6. I was responsible for caring for other family members so that it interfered with school or friendships.	1. Believes he/she is not worthy of an appropriate salary or working conditions. 2. Over performs while enabling others to underperform. 3. Stays stuck in a poor job situation. 4. Fumes silently rather than speaking up. 5. Other:_____
7. Lying was common in my family.	1. Lies to look good. 2. Has trouble distinguishing between truth and lies. 3. Gets caught in lies by coworkers or supervisors. 4. Regularly suspects that others are lying. 5. Has difficulty establishing trusting relationships with coworkers. 6. Other: _____

When I Was Growing Up:	Behaviors Now
8. I saw family members being hit or verbally abused even though I was not.	1. Feels guilty if not over performing. 2. Overworks to the point of exhaustion regularly 3. Over performs while enabling others to underperform. 4. Stays stuck in a poor job situation. 5. Underperforms given skills and talents. 6. Other:_____
9. Our family kept secrets.	1. Has difficulty establishing trusting relationships with coworkers. 2. Fearful of being "found out" as incompetent. 3. Hoards information, reluctant to share information openly. 4. Stays stuck in a poor job situation. 5. Other: _____
10. One or more family members were impaired by alcohol or drugs daily or weekly.	Anything in this "Behaviors Now" column.
11. I was hit by a family member.	1. Believes he/she is not worthy of an appropriate salary or working conditions. 2. Hits other employees or customers or throws things if enraged. 3. Stays stuck in a poor job situation. 4. Works below level of skills or talents. 5. Fumes silently rather than speaking up. 6. Other:_____

When I Was Growing Up:	Behaviors Now
12. I tried to protect others from being hit or verbally abused.	1. Feels guilty if not over performing. 2. Overworks to the point of exhaustion regularly 3. Over performs while enabling others to underperform. 4. Stays stuck in a poor job situation. 5. Believes he/she is not worthy of an appropriate salary or working conditions. 6. Works below level of skills or talents. 7. Fumes silently rather than speaking up. 8. Other: _____
13. I was sexually abused.	1. Believes he/she is not worthy of an appropriate salary or working conditions. 2. Has expectations of others that are unrealistic or unattainable because self-expectations are so high. 3. Stays stuck in a poor job situation. 4. Does not speak up when workload is overwhelming or when conditions are unreasonable. 5. Feels guilty if not over performing. 6. Overworks to point of exhaustion. 7. Is regularly involved in sexual relationships at work. 8. Has difficulty establishing trusting relationships with coworkers. 9. Needs to control every work situation to the point where others rebel. 10. Works below level of skills or talents. 11. Always wants things done his/her way only. 12. Fumes silently rather than speaking up. 13. Other: _____

When I Was Growing Up:	Behaviors Now
14. One or both of my parents had secret extramarital affairs.	1. Has difficulty establishing trusting relationships with coworkers. 2. Lies to look good. 3. Is regularly involved in sexual relationships at work. 4. Stays stuck in a poor job situation. 5. Other:_____
15. One or both of my parents were ill for a long time.	1. Needs to control every work situation to the point where others rebel. 2. Extremely uncomfortable with change or ambiguity. 3. Claims more space, supplies, or privileges than entitled to by position or work tasks. 4. Stays stuck in a poor job situation. 5. Other:_____
16. One or both of my parents died.	1. Needs to control every work situation to the point where others rebel. 2. Extremely uncomfortable with change or ambiguity. 3. Claims more space, supplies, or privileges than entitled to by position or work tasks. 4. Over performs while enabling others to underperform. 5. Stays stuck in a poor job situation. 6. Other:_____
17. We did not have enough food or clothing or housing to be physically comfortable.	1. Needs to control every work situation to the point where others rebel. 2. Extremely uncomfortable with change or ambiguity. 3. Claims more space, supplies, or privileges than entitled to by position or work tasks. 4. Stays stuck in a poor job situation. 5. Other: _____

When I Was Growing Up:	Behaviors Now
18. There was constant anger and bitterness between my parents.	1. Believes he/she is not worthy of an appropriate salary or working conditions. 2. Over performs while enabling others to underperform. 3. Stays stuck in a poor job situation. 4. Works below level of skills or talents. 5. Frequently gets locked into conflict with others. 6. Fumes silently rather than speaking up. 7. Other:_____
19. I felt like I was a spouse to my parent rather than a kid.	1. Believes he/she is not worthy of an appropriate salary or working conditions. 2. Over performs while enabling others to underperform. 3. Stays stuck in a poor job situation. 4. Works below level of skills or talents. 5. Other:_____
20. Family religious practices made it difficult to participate in school or with friends.	1. Stays stuck in a poor job situation. 2. Works below level of skills or talents. 3. Believes he/she is not worthy of an appropriate salary or working conditions. 4. Over performs while enabling others to underperform. 5. Has difficulty establishing mutual relationships with coworkers.

When I Was Growing Up:	Behaviors Now
21. A particular activity dominated my parents' lives so that they didn't pay attention to me (cleaning, shopping, TV, gambling, eating, etc.).	1. Takes credit for work of others. 2. Lets others take credit for his/her work. 3. Dominates every meeting. 4. Seeks attention through inappropriate clothing or behavior. 5. Works below level of skills or talents. 6. Overworks to the point of exhaustion regularly. 7. Other: _____
22. I was afraid of my father.	1. Fearful of males and not able to stand up for self in disagreements with men. 2. Has difficulty working with male team members. 3. Uses flirting or sexual behaviors to avoid conflict with men. 4. Behaves harshly toward coworkers and direct reports. 5. Fumes silently rather than speaking up. 6. Other:_____
23. I was afraid of my mother.	1. Fearful of women and not able to stand up for self in disagreements with women. 2. Has difficulty working with female team members. 3. Uses flirting or sexual behaviors to avoid conflict with women. 4. Behaves harshly toward coworkers and direct reports. 5. Fumes silently rather than speaking up. 6. Other:_____

When I Was Growing Up:	Behaviors Now
24. My parents were fearful of many things.	1. Needs to control every work situation to the point where others rebel. 2. Extremely uncomfortable with change or ambiguity. 3. Always wants things done his/her way only. 4. Stays stuck in a poor job situation. 5. Cannot admit to mistakes. 6. Other: _____
25. I was constantly worried that we wouldn't have enough money to get by.	1. Needs to control every work situation to the point where others rebel. 2. Extremely uncomfortable with change or ambiguity. 3. Claims more space, supplies, or privileges than entitled to by position or work tasks. 4. Always wants things done his/her way only. 5. Stays stuck in a poor job situation. 6. Works below level of skills and talents. 7. Other: _____
26. I was afraid that one or both of my parents would leave.	1. Needs to control every work situation to the point where others rebel. 2. Extremely uncomfortable with change or ambiguity. 3. Claims more space, supplies, or privileges than entitled to by position or work tasks. 4. Stays stuck in a poor job situation. 5. Always wants things done his/her way only. 6. Fumes silently rather than speaking up. 7. Over performs while enabling others to underperform. 8. Other: _____

When I Was Growing Up:	Behaviors Now
27. My family believed that women should **never** work outside the home. (For women only.)	1. Works below level of skills or talents. 2. Over performs while enabling others to underperform. 3. Has expectations of others that are unrealistic or unattainable because self-expectations are so high. 4. Overworks to the point of exhaustion regularly. 5. Cannot admit to mistakes. 6. Will not ask for help even if job is in jeopardy. 7. Believes she is not worthy of an appropriate salary or working conditions. 8. Other:_____
28. My family believed that men should **always** be the sole financial support for their families. (For men only.)	1. Stays stuck in a poor job situation. 2. Underperforms given skills and talents. 3. Has difficulty working with female team members. 4. Overworks to the point of exhaustion regularly. 5. Cannot admit to mistakes. 6. Will not ask for help even if job is in jeopardy. 7. Other: _____
29. One or more of my grandparents were addicted to alcohol or drugs.	Anything in this "Behaviors Now" column.

When I Was Growing Up:	Behaviors Now
30. My parents or other family members fought a lot.	1. Fearful that others will be angry if any disagreement is voiced. 2. Underperforms given skills and talents. 3. Extremely uncomfortable with change or ambiguity. 4. Frequently gets locked into conflict with others. 5. Hits other employees or customers or throws things if enraged. 6. Fumes silently rather than speaking up. 7. Other:_____
31. Conflict was never handled openly. Problems were shoved under the rug.	1. Fearful that others will be angry if any disagreement is voiced. 2. Does not speak up when workload is overwhelming or when conditions are unreasonable. 3. Cannot admit to mistakes. 4. Lies to look good. 5. Cannot solve problems effectively. 6. Uses flirting or sexual behaviors to avoid conflict. 7. Fumes silently rather than speaking up. 8. Other:_____
32. People teased me about how I looked or other imperfections.	1. Over performs while enabling others to underperform. 2. Lies to look good. 3. Cannot admit to mistakes. 4. Stays stuck in a poor job situation. 5. Has expectations of others that are unrealistic or unattainable because self-expectations are so high. 6. Overworks to the point of exhaustion regularly. 7. Other: _____

Look at what you circled and the "Behaviors Now" and ask yourself:

> Does this sound like me?
> Do I want things to change?
> Do I want to make different choices now?
> Do I want a different kind of life and work situation?

Not Parent Bashing

All this might sound anti-parent and family. It's not. Parenting is the hardest job anyone will ever do. I believe that most people have good intentions and parent in the best way they know how. I surely hope my children will give me that benefit of the doubt. But parents pass down to their children what was passed down to them unless they make their own conscious choices. And we have an obligation to ourselves and our own children to consciously choose what we will believe and how we will be in the world. We should not blindly accept the values, habits, and unresolved issues of those who have gone before us without consciously thinking about them. Probably much of what we have received from our families in values and behaviors is good stuff. But at least some of the coping mechanisms we learned as children will not serve us well as adults.

Options

If your life experiences have left you with some unwelcome baggage that you would like to get rid of, remember that you have a choice. You can wake up. You can take action. Start with "bibliotherapy"—find books to read yourself. You will get clearer on what might be weighing you down and holding you back. Here are some classic good books to read if you had the most wounding childhood experiences. (Don't let their publication dates fool you. There are more recent books, but none better.)

For Anyone

Bradshaw on: The Family by John Bradshaw (Deerfield Beach, FL: Health Communications, 1996).

Healing the Shame that Binds You by John Bradshaw (Deerfield Beach, FL: Health Communication, 1988).

Healing The Child Within: Discovery and Recovery for Adult Children of Dysfunctional Families by Charles Whitfield (Deerfield Beach, FL: Health Communications, 1989).

Alcohol Abuse

Alcoholics Anonymous Big Book (4th edition) by Alcoholics Anonymous World Services, Inc. (2001).

Codependents' Guide to the Twelve Steps by Melody Beattie (New York: Simon and Schuster, 1990).

The Complete ACOA Sourcebook: Adult Children of Alcoholics at Home, at Work and in Love by Janet Woititz (Deerfield Beach: Health Communications, 2002).

One Day at a Time in Al-Anon, Al-Anon Family Group Head, Inc., Virginia Beach, VA, (1984).

Sexual Abuse

Beginning to Heal: A First Book for Men and Women Who Were Sexually Abused As Children by Ellen Bass and Laura Davis (New York: HarperCollins, 2003).

In addition to bibliotherapy, find in your community a therapist or counselor to work with you either one-on-one or in a therapeutic group. Counseling or support groups can be very helpful.

If you don't like the therapist you first go to, try another one and keep moving till you find a therapist that you trust and who helps you move forward in your life. Read Sara's story in Chapter 5 and you will see that she didn't give up on professional help even when she didn't like the first two therapists she tried. The third one was just right for her. Therapists are people, after all, and not every therapist will be a good match for you.

The place where you work may have an employee assistance office. In almost every case, the services are provided at no charge and the counselors can help you find therapists or groups in your community. Ask up front what the confidentiality policy is. Most employee assistance offices will help you with any problem that is impacting your ability to do your job.

The odds of recovering from alcohol addiction without professional help or regular recovery meetings are one in fifty thousand.[75] If life has become unmanageable because of alcohol or drugs, go to your phone book and find the number for Alcoholics Anonymous. A recorded message will tell you the meeting times and places. You can also find a meeting at http://www.aa.org/en_find_meeting.cfm. Chances are good that there's a regular meeting in your area. At AA you will receive the most nonjudgmental welcome you can imagine.

Did you grow up with someone with a drug or alcohol problem or is someone in your family or home or circle of friends struggling with it now? If so, go to a meeting of Al-Anon, the organization for families and friends of alcohol or drug addicts. You can find a meeting anywhere in the United States and Canada at http://www.al-anonfamilygroups.org/meetings/meeting.html. At an Al-Anon meeting, as well, you will find welcoming and nonjudgmental people. In both AA and Al-Anon, anonymity for those who attend meetings is a cherished principle

AA and Al-Anon do not provide counseling, but rather mutual support for living a different kind of life without the substances and all that goes with them. The other members will not typically give you advice, but will listen to what you have to say with open hearts and will share their own experiences with you.

Reflection

When you were a child growing up, you didn't have a lot of choices. You do now. Maya Angelou is credited with saying: "You did what you knew how to do, and when you knew better, you did better."[76]

CHAPTER 5:
WHAT MAKES
ORGANIZATIONS SICK?

The best we can do, then, in response to our incomprehensible and dangerous world, is to practice holding equilibrium internally—*no matter what insanity is transpiring out there.*

— Elizabeth Gilbert in *Eat, Pray, Love*[77]

Most U.S. organizations are sick. Some companies, agencies, organizations, and institutions have sniffles and some are terminally ill.[78] To define what I mean by "sick," let's think healthy first and then flip it over.

Healthy

Think of a healthy human body. (It makes sense to compare an organization, especially an incorporated body of any kind, to the human body.) Here are some characteristics of a healthy body:

- Functioning to capacity—does what it is theoretically capable of doing;
- Processes work like they are supposed to and show the expected results;

111

- Able to repair—when things do go wrong, mending is quick and predictable;
- Protected by immune system—able to prevent illness—the organization isn't consistently laid low by unanticipated problems;
- Parts work in harmony;
- Integrity—No essential parts are missing.

Note that income and profits are not part of the list, because, as important as they are, they are the outcome of a healthy organization. Ken Blanchard says, "Profit is the applause you get for taking care of your customers and creating a motivating environment for your people."[79]

Sick

When I think of a sick organization, I think of an organization that does not consistently show those healthy characteristics and instead is more likely to demonstrate:

- Functioning below capacity—the organization is not living up to its potential to create positive outcomes for consumers, stockholders, workers, or communities;
- Dysfunction—technical or human processes are illogical, overly complex, or poorly executed, producing disappointing results;
- Inability to repair—when things do go wrong, mending is slow and accompanied by the gangrene of festering emotions;

- Compromised immune system—if there's a problem in the air, the organization catches it—it is so worn out that small incidents or problems turn into big complications.
- Parts compete with one another for resources—materials, people, technology, space, dollars.
- Essential parts are missing or worn out, causing fatigue and extraordinary wear and tear on other parts.

Not every organization will exhibit all the symptoms of illness, but it takes only one or two to cripple the organization and make it a difficult place to work within.

Why Are They Sick?

A man's transformation from a husband, lover, father, and responsible adult community member when he enters the plant is described in an untitled poem circulated among auto workers. The poignant poem gained a national audience when it appeared in Peters & Waterman's *In Search of Excellence*.

> For eight hours
> You shall be different.
> What is it that instantaneously makes
> A child out of a man?[80]

What makes children out of adults when they go to work is our belief system about people, organizations, and the best way to get work done. Most of the dysfunction that routinely happens in businesses and agencies, and associations—arrogant communication, abusive supervisors, employees who cover up their

113

mistakes, sabotage of others, secrecy, bullying, and the list goes on and on—occurs because of our fundamental beliefs about work and organizations.

If we could change what we believe, we could improve the health and productivity of our businesses and organizations. I don't see that happening soon. That is why The Clover Practice™ is important to anyone who works in one of these organizations and wants to stay healthy in his or her mind and spirit. As individuals, we can't much change the basic assumptions of our organizations, but we can modify our own assumptions and shape our own behavior along healthy lines.

Three culprits affect the health of most organizations in the United States. One is a set of beliefs, one is a practice, and one is a predisposition. The last two arise from the first one. The three culprits are the following:

1. The belief that a patriarchal, hierarchical organization with command and control tactics is the best way to ensure good work;
2. Too many people without the skills and appropriate motives supervise others;
3. Willingness to maintain illusions.

Culprit #1: Patriarchy, Hierarchy, Control

Culprit #1 is the belief that a patriarchal, hierarchical organization with command and control tactics is the best way to ensure good work. Consider the most common form of economic organization—the corporation. The corporation is structured in a hierarchy with those at the top having power to decide the future of the organization (on behalf of the stockholders) and those at the bottom having little or no say in organizational fate and receiving the least financial benefit. Marjorie Kelly writes of employees, "They are not citizens of corporate society, but subjects."[81] (Step back and think about how strange it is that a company can be bought and sold without a word to the employees who make it what it is.) We are so accustomed to this organization that we don't even question how such an antiquated form of organization, which hearkens to the days of kings, is the dominant economic organizer in a democratic society. The rules of accounting were written in the fifteenth century![82] When kings ruled the nations of the world, the assumption was that there was a direct line of authority from God down to the king, down to the nobility, down to the common people. This view of authority hasn't changed much in the world of business. The corporation is and always has been, built on the basis of patriarchy with all the assumptions that go along with patriarchy, some of which include:

- People at the top of the organization are smarter than those at the bottom, do not need to consult with them, and should, in fact, control them;
- People must be told what to do;
- People at the top of the organization are more deserving than those at the bottom and thus are entitled to a variety of privileges;
- People need to be watched, constantly, by those in authority because they cannot be trusted; and

- White male inclinations and worldviews are superior to female inclinations and worldviews (e.g., competition versus cooperation).

Even nonprofit organizations with no stockholders to report to are organized along the same hierarchical lines as corporations with a board that selects the executive director and makes policy decisions for the organization.[83]

Author Peter Block says that the patriarchal system of organization that we have inherited is based on the "belief that it is those at the top who are responsible for the success of the organization and the well-being of its members...We govern our organizations by valuing above all else, consistency, control, and predictability."[84]

Elizabeth Dodson Gray adds to Block's description of patriarchy the element of a male-dominated view of how the world works. She says that what we take for granted as reality "has come to us through the eyes and ears, hearts and minds, images and perceptions—in short, the life experience—of the male."[85]

Gray calls patriarchy a "conceptual trap." Conceptual traps, she says, are not consistent with reality, but they persist because we cannot see them. "A conceptual trap is a way of thinking that is like a room that, once you are in it, you cannot imagine a world outside."[86] I have spent a lot of time thinking about which came first—patriarchy or hierarchy—and finally decided that they are inseparable.

The assumption that people at the top are better able to make decisions than people closest to the work is also firmly rooted in the "scientific management" principles of Frederick W. Taylor who wrote and worked at the beginning of the twentieth century. Taylor championed the model of a workplace where some people did all the thinking and some people did all the work. For example, Taylor says, "...The man suited to handling pig iron is too stupid to properly train himself."[87] As the biographer of Taylor says, scientific management "so permeates the soil of modern life we no longer realize it's there."[88]

To be sure, there are organizations that exhibit healthy behaviors and sincere managers and leaders who inspire and support while producing great results. But *Fortune*'s "100 Best Companies to Work For" are a mere 100 among millions. We have collectively and largely unconsciously decided that the best way to get work done in organizations is through patriarchy, hierarchy, and control. Alternate views such as partnership, stewardship, and genuinely shared decision making—all of which require redistribution of power throughout the organization—have scarcely been attempted. Companies like Google, Gore, Costco, and Patagonia that follow a different paradigm are written about in management journals and books because they are so unusual.

The unconscious assumptions in the workplace, such as the view that those in management are the parents and the rest are dependent children, must be held by everyone in order for these to stick. Peter Block writes elegantly about how we have all made unspoken choices, such as the choice between feeling dependent or empowered. "Dependency also holds those above personally responsible for how we feel about ourselves...and how much freedom we have...Dependence is the collusion required for patriarchy and parenting to endure."[89] The system of patriarchy and hierarchy puts managers in a predicament as well when those they supervise look to them (impossibly) as the source of all good things. People give their bosses a huge amount of power over them in this parent-child model, Peter Block says. "Managers are not the Wizard of Oz."[90]

Parker Palmer, a noted educator, points out that we have taught people to be passive, starting with their schooling. "When students spend year after year as passive recipients of education, small wonder they carry their passivity into the workplace. They have not learned, because we did not teach them, that opening one's mouth to challenge what is wrong is a way to stay sane, honor their own integrity, and live by their deepest callings."[91]

We do not serve other adults when we take responsibility for their well-being.

– Peter Block[92]

Our economic system requires that we sell our labor for cash. This is a relatively new development in human history. Only with the Industrial Revolution of the midnineteenth century, has it come to pass that the majority of people sell their labor to get what they need to live. (In the age of agriculture, people produced most of what they needed to live without "going somewhere" to work.) We must wake up to the fact that the vast majority of the organizations in the United States were founded on patriarchal principles that are very much at odds with democracy. It is a built-in disconnect. Business author Joel Henning echoes this theme, writing of Americans' fierce commitment to individual rights of expression and the pursuit of life, liberty, and happiness. "Yet when we enter the factory door or the lobby of the business cathedrals in our major cities, we leave our belief in democratic principles in the car."[93]

The centralized power of most workplaces clashes with beliefs we hold dear as Americans. We send our young men and women to fight and die for the very ideals that are trashed daily in the workplace. This paradox is a setup for all involved. We will not be able to live and work as healthy adults until we can wake up, step back, and see what we are dealing with.

Culprit #2: Inadequate Managerial Skills and Motives

Culprit #2 is the fact that too many people who don't have adequate skills or appropriate attitudes supervise other people. I am appalled that we have made a distinction between managing and leading. We think of managers as people who keep a lid on things and make sure that everyone follows the rules, and we feature leaders as those who think great thoughts and have extraordinary vision and charisma. If you accept responsibility for what happens to people during the majority of their waking hours, and if your decisions affect their material well-being, you had better have some leadership in you, regardless of your title. Every manager should be a leader, but too many people supervise others without qualifications of mind or spirit.

"…At least 55 percent of managers in American corporations are unfit for their jobs," says psychologist Robert Hogan who has administered over a million personality tests over thirty years.[94] On the darker side, psychologists at Multi Health Systems in Ontario who administer the Business Scan 360 personality screening test claim that nearly one in fifty managers can be classified as psychopathic. "Sub-criminal psychopaths show up more in management ranks than elsewhere in companies," they say.[95] Robert Hare, the psychologist who created the standard clinical test for psychopathy, is cocreator (with Paul Babiak) of the Business Scan 360. Hare says that psychopaths are "…without conscience and incapable of empathy, guilt, or loyalty to anyone but themselves."[96] In their book, *Snakes in Suits: When Psychopaths Go to Work,* Babiak and Hare say that people with psychotic behaviors are more likely to ascend to leadership in today's organizations because they will be able to operate without being recognized in organizations going through rapid and chaotic change due to unprecedented economic and social pressures.[97]

The patriarchal "command and control" hierarchy *demands* multiple levels of supervisors. Our beliefs about what makes organizations solid requires a layer of people whose job it is to watch and direct others.[98] In today's knowledge economy, it is more and more common that individual workers know much more about their work than those who supervise them. Yet we cling to the idea that we need bosses with a wide range of authority over the work of those they supervise. And although many organizations have made valiant attempts to flatten their hierarchies and allow decision making to take place closer to where the work is done, the underlying beliefs and assumptions about power and control have not changed much. We just have smaller kingdoms.

The prevailing belief is that management is a class rather than a function.[99] This view of management as a superior class of people makes trust difficult, partnership impossible, and automatically pits managers against those they supervise. Innovation—the lifeblood of any modern organization—will be difficult in these circumstances.

I have had the privilege of working with some of the best leaders on the planet. They approach others with respect and are able to mobilize people around a shared vision of what the clients or customers or students or stakeholders need. To be that kind of outstanding leader, they have had to "work around" the existing system and often do downright miraculous things without a lot of support from "the system." It would be easier for them personally sometimes, if they didn't always take the high road of service, respect, and quality. But, of course, they cannot be less than they are.

It is not that we don't need people to manage and lead. We will always need people who keep everyone focused on innovation and common goals and who provide a central place to go to with ideas and problems that cross over units. We need someone who can help coordinate multiple groups and activities and distribute resources appropriately to the work at hand. We need someone who has a view of and is concerned for the whole. But this requires particular skills and attitudes, not a crown, as one writer put it.

When someone is good at what he or she does, it is a common practice to elevate that individual to the class of manager. This elevation happens on the assumption that the individual who is good at his or her job will be equally good at helping other people do their jobs. In most organizations, becoming a manager is the only way to make more money.

We know that management requires a set of skills that most people are not born with—excellent communication skills and especially the ability to listen, the ability to look beyond the details to the big picture, a willingness to look at processes and procedures when things go wrong rather than looking right away for whom to blame, the ability to apologize and forgive, and a willingness to share credit and blame to name a few. These need to be developed by most people. As long as we view management as an entitlement or reward, we can never admit how much help people really need to be good managers. In today's business environment with human resources and training budgets slashed, even less training and succession planning for leaders is available. What is left for teaching new generations of leaders is the people in those roles now, serving as models. Let's hope that they are good models.

Culprit #3: Organizational Illusions

Culprit #3 is the willingness of organizations to maintain illusions. An illusion is a false or misleading impression of reality. James Lucas says, "Illusion comes when we perceive something to be true that isn't true or is only partly true. Illusion comes because we want to believe the thing is true. Illusion is often—perhaps always—tied into false hope."[100] The problem with organizational illusions is that they tend to produce more illusions and prevent the real issues and problems from being addressed.[101]

Organizational illusions are many and varied, but here are some common examples:

- Families are [invisible and] not our problem.

This means that care of children is not the concern of the employer and that it is in fact the concern of female workers (usually) who have to figure it out for themselves. What would happen if every family where both parents work decided that one would stay home to care for the children? Would employers feel the pinch? Yes. Indeed, many organizations would not be able to function. Even without such a drastic change, how much productivity is lost because parents have no way to care for sick children other than to stay home from work? Yet we continue with policies that guarantee hardship for parents and children and a veritable void of childcare.

- We want a diverse workforce, student body, or clientele.

Although it is expedient to talk about a diverse workplace, it is common for organizations to simultaneously pass over potential employees who "aren't like us" or "won't fit the culture here." In the higher education world, for example, it is not uncommon to find sincere efforts to attract minority faculty, staff, and students to campuses but without any attention to creating a welcoming or supportive environment for them.

- We communicate well around here.

"The single biggest problem in communication is the illusion that it has taken place," George Bernard Shaw says.[102] I am always struck by how much effort it takes to really get a message heard. Each of us is so bombarded with information, advertising, data, messages—both paper and electronic—that we generally need to read, see and hear about something more than once for it to really grab our attention. I hear statements such as "They know about that. Everyone got a notice in their mailbox!" A one-time announcement is an illusion of communication. International consultant Steve Denning says, "When speakers forget or ignore the interactive nature of communication, as frequently occurs in organizations where speakers mistake their hierarchical power over their employees for an actual capacity to force listeners to listen, the outcome is predictably disastrous."[103]

Many leaders avoid telling employees any kind of bad news, thinking they can thus control people's fear. Lucas reminds us that "...it's the *not* sharing it that scares them to death."[104]

Meg Wheatley describes organizations with rigid chains of command that prevent people from talking to anyone outside their immediate department, "... in most companies, protocols define who can be consulted, advised, or criticized. We are afraid of what would happen if we let these elements of the organization recombine, reconfigure, or speak truthfully to one another. We are afraid that things will fall apart."[105]

- Our Salaries Are Confidential

In many organizations, there is an unwritten rule that employee salaries are confidential and not to be discussed with fellow employees. Sometimes the rule is written—over a third of companies responding to an online survey said they had policies forbidding employees from discussing their salaries.[106] (It has actually been illegal to forbid discussions of pay since 1935.)[107] But the illusion comes in when anyone believes that people don't know what their coworkers make. People talk whether they are supposed to or not. And while there are strong arguments for making salaries an open matter, one of the arguments in favor is that it would dispel the illusion of secrecy. Nothing stays secret for long in organizations.

You can probably think of illusions that are alive and well in your workplace. If everyone followed the first principle of The Clover Practice™, Tell the Truth, Always, organizations would not be able to maintain illusions, at least not for long. Eckhart Tolle writes, "If you recognize illusion as illusion, it dissolves…Its survival depends on your mistaking it for reality."[108] The healthier an organization is, the more likely it is to recognize when things aren't working, to admit when mistakes have been made, and set about to make things right while learning as much as possible from what went wrong.

Life sells illusion by the truckload. But we don't have to buy.

– James Lucas[109]

Sick organizations are more likely to continue down paths that aren't working out as well as expected, to blame the wrong people while shielding those who should assume responsibility, and to give the appearance of solving problems without actually doing so. Worrying more about how things look rather than what is actually happening is not the behavior of a healthy person or group. The sicker an organization is, the more willing it will be to maintain illusions.

There are plenty of other reasons why organizations have problems—the economy, supply and demand, global competition, undercapitalization, loss of funding, and the fact that some workers don't give a hoot. The three culprits described here, however, seem to be consistent across industries, organizations, and institutions.

Organizations That Make You Sick

Chronic stress from workplaces makes people sick. Researchers have found that greater levels of job stress increase people's chances of developing metabolic syndrome, which is linked to the development of heart disease and type 2 diabetes as well as other illnesses.[110] Chronic stress also depresses the immune system.[111]

Workers who are dissatisfied with their jobs are more likely to become ill, according to the largest-ever study of the relationship between job satisfaction and physical and mental well-being carried out in the UK.[112] Thus the sicker the organization is and the more stress it causes, the more likely it is to make you sick.

Reflection

The Clover Practice™ gives you the tools to step back from an unhealthy work situation (that has problems automatically built into it—patriarchy and hierarchy, unprepared or unfit managers, and too many illusions) and ask yourself some important questions:

- Is this a place where I can practice honesty and maintain my personal integrity?
- Are there others who want our workplace to be a healthy and productive environment for everyone?
- Are people treated in a way that acknowledges our mutual interdependence?
- Is this an environment that I want to continue to contribute to?
- Do I need to find a healthier place to work?

If you answered yes to the last question, the next chapter is for you.

CHAPTER 6:
WHEN IT'S TIME TO
MAKE A CHANGE

When you follow your bliss...
doors will open where you would not have thought there
would be doors; and where there wouldn't be a door for
anyone else.

— Joseph Campbell[113]

Taking Control of Your Life

Several years ago a friend of mine died, a friend who was younger than I, and more talented, and more credentialed. What I remember her most for is the gorgeous, over-the-top luscious cakes she brought to potluck dinners. How can she be gone? What would she have done differently? Would she have worked harder? (I don't think she could have.) Would she have baked more fabulous cakes?

Her death is a reminder to me. This is the only life we have for now on earth. We have to make it count. We can't waste it. Don't waste your life in a miserable job.

If the place where you work now makes it difficult for you to live The Clover Practice™—if people are penalized for being straightforward or if the culture is one of fear or if people are treated as if they are machine parts—consider making a change.

Most people have more career and job options than they think they have. What holds people back from seeking better work situations? Let's tick off the biggie first—fear. We fear loss, change, the unknown. We fear ending up in a worse situation, making less money.

The fear is understandable given that over two million people have lost jobs since 2000. However, people are still getting hired. Every month in the United States, from 1,250,000 to 2,500,000 job slots become vacant in the "musical chairs" process of people changing jobs and retiring. And that figure does not include new jobs created.[114] Employment, like everything else, is cyclical. Even if you aren't ready to make a leap right now, you can be preparing yourself for when the time is right.

The second reason people stay in jobs that are literally or figuratively killing them is L-A-Z-I-N-E-S-S. To change jobs or careers, you are going to have to make changes in your life. It can seem easier to stay in a job that is boring, unreasonably demanding, dangerous, demeaning, low paying, demoralizing, dishonest—you name it—than to get moving.

For parents, especially single parents, the burden of working and raising children can be overwhelming. I was a single working parent for a time and what I remember most is always being exhausted. During that time, I worked in two different organizations, one a classic sick organization and, later, a much healthier organization. It made a big difference. I was still tired when I worked in the second, healthier place, but I was able to enjoy the time I had with my daughter much more when I got home from work because I wasn't worn down from craziness. Even if you are doing that superhuman job of single parenting, you owe it to yourself and your children not to stay in a sick organization. If you put up with it, what are you teaching your children? On the other hand, consider the lesson you are teaching when you prepare yourself to move on and then do it.

> *Our growth requires that we step away from the crowd, even if it scares us to do it.*
>
> – Marsha Sinetar[115]

Margaret Lulic's book *Who We Could Be at Work* includes thirty-five interviews of individuals who made purposeful changes. She shows that people can and do make changes, often after years in one position or organization. Lulic says, "We'd like to go home from work knowing we've made a contribution…We'd like to go home feeling valued…Many of us feel as if much of what we have to offer is wasted in the workplace. And it's hard to find the time or the spirit to be who we'd like to be in the rest of our lives."[116]

As described earlier, since our economic system is capitalism, we literally sell our labor every day to get the capital (money) we need to buy food, clothing, shelter, housing, transportation, medical care, and amusement. None of us can make everything we need to live. The closest most of us come to that is planting a garden, sewing our own garments, and riding our bikes. You are selling your labor to your employer. Are you getting a good deal? Are you getting a good return in terms of satisfaction, self-respect, and dollars?

Right Livelihood and Your Calling

"Right livelihood" is a concept from Buddhism that can help you decide whether or not you need to make a job or career change. Right livelihood is work that is "consciously chosen, done with full awareness and care and leading to enlightenment."[117] It is work that you enjoy for the most part and that makes use of your talents and abilities. Right livelihood engages you in work that is aligned with your reasons for being on this earth.

> *Remember, you were put on this earth to do something wonderful with your life. You have within you talents and abilities so vast that you could never use them all...*
> – Brian Tracy[118]

The Puritan work ethic that is so much a part of American culture is based on the idea that we must work as punishment for sin. The Old Testament of the Bible says, "By the sweat of your brow you will eat your food until you return to the ground..."[119] Buddha offers a different view of work as activity that can bring us fulfillment and contentment as well as a paycheck. Kahlil Gibran says, "Work is love made visible."[120] If we looked at work, not as punishment, but as activity that can help us grow spiritually and emotionally, as Buddha describes it (enlightenment), would we stay where we are?

> *So many people walk around with a meaningless life. They seem half asleep even when they're busy doing things they think are important. This is because they're chasing the wrong things.*
> – Morrie Schwartz from *Tuesdays With Morrie*[121]

Most of us don't use the word "vocation" anymore, in everyday conversation, although it's certainly around and is generally understood to relate to working. In Latin, the word "vocare" means "to call." In medieval times, people believed that careers in the service of God and the church "called" to people who had been divinely chosen. Today the idea of a calling has expanded to all kinds of careers. Business psychologists Timothy Butler and James Waldroop advise business executives on career strategies. Butler says that although people use the words "vocation," "career" and "job" interchangeably, they are different. "Vocation is the most profound of the three, and it has to do with your calling. It's what you're doing in life that makes a difference for you, that builds meaning for you, that you can look back on in your later years to see the impact you've made on the world."[122]

Butler says that people who want to change their employment situation need to pay attention more to what deeply interests them and not blindly do what they happen to be good at.[123]

Rick Jarow, PhD, is an associate professor of religious studies at Vassar College and creator of the internationally known workshops "Creating the Work You Love," which are known alternatively as "Anticareer Workshops." He starts his workshops with questions like these: "What do you do easily, naturally, effortlessly? What do you care about? What makes you indignant enough to change yourself and/or the world?"[124]

Jarow encourages us to think in terms of abundance rather than scarcity as we are more inclined to do. His goal is to help people

133

connect their inner sense of abundance and feelings and only then set career-related goals. His emphasis on exploring this inner space first is where the "anticareer" idea comes from. He says, "The work you love is created when you really connect with your creative wisdom and are willing to listen to how it communicates directly to you."[125]

> *There is a place that needs you and a place where you need to be. See these two coming together.*
> – Hilda Charlton, quoted by Rick Jarow[126]

Jarow says there is a spiritual and mystical element of finding what Buddha describes as "right livelihood." He says, "There are forces at work that we cannot even begin to conceive of. More often than not, we draw the circumference of possibility too tight around our limited ideas."[127]

Dream Your Dreams

Now what about you? What are your deep interests? What kinds of activities can you get lost in for hours without even noticing that time is passing? If you didn't have to go to your current job every day, what would you like to do? In Table 6.1, make a list of the activities, tasks, and hobbies that really bring you happiness:

Table 6.1. What I Really Enjoy Doing

Very likely these are the things that "call you." Think about how a different work or career situation could enable you to do these things more often or more consistently. Could you make money doing these things? If you don't have a clue, take this list to a career counselor at your local community college and ask for ideas.

If you are still not sure about what your "true calling" might be, Brian Tracy, a human development expert, suggests asking people who are closest to you. "Ask them 'What do you think I would be the very best at doing with my life?' It is absolutely amazing how people around you, including your spouse, your best friends, and your parents, can see clearly what you should be doing when often you cannot see it yourself."[128]

Really do it. Ask someone (or several people) close to you, "If I could change my work situation, what do you think I would be the very best at doing?" Record your answers in Table 6.2. Don't forget to add your reactions to the suggestions.

Table 6.2. Family and Friends' Views

1. My family and friends tell me I am good at:

- _____
- _____
- _____
- _____
- _____
- _____
- _____
- _____

2. Does what people told you feel like a good fit for you?

_____
_____
_____

3. What ideas does this give you for next steps?

_____
_____
_____

A recent article on change says that only one in ten people who have had coronary bypass surgery actually make changes in their lifestyles "even at the risk of dying."[129] Writer Alan Deutschman concludes that fear is not a great motivator for change, but that "positive visions of the future are a much stronger inspiration than fear."[130] That is why it is so important for you to have a clear vision of what you want for your work and life rather than just hoping that things will get better. To that extent, dream about what you want to do with your talents, imagine yourself in a different work setting, talk to people doing work you are interested in. Write in Table 6.3 about how it would feel if tomorrow you were doing what you want to do with your time and your life.

Table 6.3. The Ideal Future for Me

1. If I were doing what I really want to do with my life, this is what I would be doing:
   _____
   _____
   _____

2. This is how I would feel:
   _____
   _____

3. This is how my typical day would go:
   Morning _____
   _____
   _____

   Afternoon _____
   _____
   _____

   Evening _____
   _____
   _____

Three Smashing Successes

You may have recognized that you are working in an organization that is not healthy. You may work in an organization that does not look anything like those described in Chapter 5 and still have a yearning to make a change. Others have done it and you can too.

Here are three stories of people I know personally (not their real names). All of them were unhappy with their work lives and wanted to make a change. There were no guarantees for any of them that they would find something better or something that paid as much as what they were making. But they were motivated to find work that was more satisfying and more in tune with their souls. They wanted to feel peaceful at the end of the workday.

Janie

Janie is a fifty-something woman who worked in a civil service position for most of her adult life. She began as a clerical worker and rose to the highest level she could as an administrative assistant. Her life was not easy. When her first marriage ended, she was a single parent with two daughters. Although she struggled with alcohol, she achieved sobriety on her own. She sometimes worked more than one job to make enough to support herself and her children. She adored her two daughters and made a welcoming, comfortable home for them. In her forties, she was fortunate to find a funny, loving man who taught her the art and love of fishing. Soon the two married.

Janie had a deep pool of creativity in her soul and an artistic eye. She had a special talent for publication design and discovered the therapeutic benefits of knitting. She decorated her office with flowers and colorful art objects. However, she was not happy with her job. Her work did not give her satisfaction or peace of mind and she seldom had the feeling that she had accomplished all she felt she needed to. She worried about the job in her off hours. The tension increased. She said that in spite of her efforts, nothing seemed to turn things around.

Then the worst thing that could happen to a parent happened—her twenty-one-year-old daughter died unexpectedly of a congenital brain aneurism. Several days later her father passed away. Janie was shattered and as she herself said, life would never be the same.

It was at this low point in her life, grieving the loss of her precious daughter and father and dealing with a job that was falling apart, that she decided to make a change for herself. Job hunting without a college degree in a college town with a very highly educated workforce was challenging. She did not let that stop her. She applied for a half dozen positions, determined to find employment that worked for her. And she found it. She is working in a different state agency, doing work she loves. (She recently was even sent to the East Coast to staff a business trip.) With her new sense of peacefulness about work, Janie is devoting herself to something that has become dear to her heart—supporting the cause of organ donation. I asked her if she thought she had changed after finding a new workplace, especially after being in the same environment for so many years. "Yes," she said, "I've come to realize that life is a journey. It is up to me to learn from my experiences and move forward. I am richer for doing so—richer in knowledge and self-worth. I will continue to learn. That is the joy of living."

Fritz

Fritz was just about to turn fifty when he decided his job had become unbearable. He had been working since the age of sixteen and had held many kinds of jobs. He was smart and gifted with mechanical ability and could do anything that required knowledge of how things work. If it had gears, wheels, screws, and plugs, he could fix it.

In his twenties, he had begun a career as a paramedic firefighter, work that he loved. He speaks wistfully of the adrenaline rush he would get driving a thirty-eight-foot ladder truck to a fire with lights flashing and siren screaming. He remembered fighting house fires in below-zero weather when icicles would form on his eyebrows and mustache and it would take hours to get warm afterward. He remembered the people he saved with CPR and his medical skills. He remembered people he wasn't able to save, but whose families were still grateful to him for his compassion.

When he got into his forties, the physical demands—scrambling up and down ladders and jarring awake in the middle of the night to rush to a car accident—these were getting harder and harder. An opportunity presented itself to work in the field of medical data and he took it. Making the decision to leave work he loved for work that was better for him physically was soul wrenching. And even after he had made the change and went in to work in a shirt and tie every day, his children's disappointment pained him. "Daddy, aren't you going to be a fireman anymore?"

In his move to an office job, he learned everything he could about the business side of health care. Marriage to a woman who lived in another state meant a move and yet another job change. He soon found a position that combined his interest in data, computers, and health care. He headed a three-person team responsible for working with a client agency. He adored his team members and they him.

His problem was the client to which the team was assigned. The client group included a couple of longtime leaders who resisted his efforts to automate their data system—the very thing Fritz was assigned to do. He would bring solutions to them and they would reject them out of hand. They seldom returned his calls or e-mails and their words and body language in meetings said they didn't want anything his team had to offer. They did, however, have frequent potluck lunch meetings, which greatly annoyed Fritz. "If I have to look at another seven-layer salad, I am going to kill myself," he said, not laughing.

This situation found him awake at 3:00 a.m. watching reruns, trying desperately to get to sleep. He couldn't enjoy spending time with his family because the hopelessness of this job situation kept replaying in his head. He wasn't excited about another job or career change, but when his doctor prescribed tranquilizers for him, he decided it was time to act.

> *"If I have to look at another seven-layer salad, I am going to kill myself," he said, not laughing.*

He made an appointment with a personal coach and consultant who specializes in helping adults make midlife career changes. The coach, hearing of his wide range of experiences, said, "You should try some consulting. You have a lot to offer." Fritz put his qualifications on a national online job site and within two weeks was on a plane to another state as a consultant. He hasn't stopped yet and that was eight years ago. Fritz has worked in half a dozen states, flies home Thursday evenings, and makes more money than he ever dreamed he could.

Sara

Sara looks like she just stepped out of a fashion magazine. She is a stunning twenty-something woman of color. And in her short life, she has already made a deliberate decision to leave an unhealthy work environment. Her first professional position after graduating with a bachelor's degree was not going well. She was a student advisor in a program for at risk students. Her problems with the position fell into three general categories. The first was a poor fit between her personal values and the organization. She had worked hard to get an education and believed that students in the program should be held more accountable for their grades and behavior.

The second problem was the lack of boundaries on the workday. During peak times, she and others were expected to work from 7:00 a.m. till 11:00 p.m. and the workday often stretched to 1:00 a.m. if students got into trouble or had problems. The third dimension of the problem was fallout from tension between her supervisor and the head of the program.

"I felt so stuck," she said. "I thought it would never end. I can laugh about it now, but then I thought I would be stuck in that job forever." For months, she couldn't even consider leaving. She worried it would ruin her reputation and that she would never find another job after leaving her first professional position. "I was so afraid. I don't even know what I was afraid of. I was just afraid. I wondered if I was going crazy."

The work situation was taking its toll on her health. She is a slender woman, but lost thirteen pounds from nausea and vomiting induced by the stressful work situation. Her fiancé said, "If you come home one more time crying, I'm going up there myself!" Sara hadn't realized till that moment how her job misery was affecting him. "I didn't want us to end up on the evening news, so I decided that something had to change."

Shortly afterward, her supervisor stormed into her office reeking of alcohol, slammed the door and stood against it, barring her from leaving. He demanded that she come with him to discuss a problem. She refused to go with him and called for assistance. She left the office and applied for a short-term leave of absence, which was granted.

Leaving the environment that had been the source of so much pain for her did not immediately give her peace. "I was depressed. I cried a lot. I thought my reputation was ruined and that I had no skills or anything to offer anyone. I stayed home waiting for interviews. My depression was definitely affecting my relationship with my fiancé." After two months of limbo, she landed another professional position in a prestigious office. Even then, she did not enjoy peace of mind. "At first I felt so uptight and paranoid. I felt hugely in debt to my employers because they had been my savior by hiring me." Fortunately, she remained in therapy, which helped her see how much she had to offer her new employers. (She tried two therapists before finding a third whom she felt comfortable talking to.) Looking back on the year and a half she had spent in the dysfunctional work situation, she said, "I stayed way too long."

Has she changed as a result of all of this? "I am not afraid anymore. I have learned that just because someone is your supervisor doesn't mean they are god. I am not afraid to say what I honestly think. Others do, so I don't know why I can't." Sara said she realized that she needed to have some savings so she would not feel she was "at the mercy of a job." The health problems that began in the first job never completely went away, but she is a different person now, she says. "I would leave in a heartbeat if anything like that ever happened to me again."

Education

The rest of this chapter includes resources to help you achieve the goals you have set or will set for yourself for a more satisfying work life, starting with education. A job change may require getting additional education. This might mean a course or two, not necessarily a degree. Even twenty years ago, it wasn't that easy for adults, once they were working and had families, to get more education. That has changed. Colleges and universities have child care centers. Working adults are able to take courses and even get degrees completely through the Internet. See University of Phoenix or Western Governors University as examples of online degree opportunities.

> *You are selling your labor to your employer. Are you getting a good deal?*

Community colleges and technical colleges have blossomed in every state and offer tremendous resources for people who want to better their work and personal lives. A recent article describes the phenomenon of baby boomers enrolling in community colleges, "changing gears and retraining for new jobs that are less physically taxing."[131] The article features a man who formerly delivered Wonder Bread and Hostess cakes who has retrained (via community college) as a surgical technologist. Another man who worked construction is finishing his college degree so he can work in an office environment. A fifty-three-year-old electrician is retraining to start his own electrical business.[132] Most community colleges offer free career services to help you figure out what courses fit your interests and talents. The educational opportunities are there for you.

Moving Around in Your Organization

Often overlooked is the fact that even within the same organization, there can be vastly different work cultures. A position change doesn't necessarily mean leaving the organization in which you work now. Perhaps just switching offices or units would be a big improvement. Find out who is retiring or where new jobs are opening up in your own organization. Make a conscious effort to find out where there might be opportunities for you. Rick Jarow says, "Do you dream of expressing your strongest values, energies, and talents through your work...? All too often we bury such dreams in busyness and obligations, pretending that we have no alternatives to our current jobs or careers. But we do have alternatives—if we are willing to throw off the conditioned role of being a victim of circumstance."[133]

Some organizations offer in-house internships or opportunities to work for a short time in another part of the organization. This is free learning. Take advantage of it if you are unhappy where you are. If such a program is not available, ask if you can do some "benchmarking" with other organizations to learn how they handle particular processes or problems. For example, if you want to learn about best practices in customer service, visit with management of a successful hotel or store. This will give you a sense of perspective and an idea of what's out there. Not knowing your choices is a big barrier to even considering a change.

Start Your Own Business

More and more people who find organizational life intolerable are starting their own businesses. Over the past decade, on average, 465,000 people launched new businesses every month.[134] The vast majority of these were small businesses, employing fewer than one hundred people. Many were tiny businesses employing one or two people. Every state has a Small Business Development Center that provides information and classes to help people decide on starting a business and then supports ongoing operations. All the information and some of the classes are free.

Even people who started small businesses that didn't succeed long term usually say they were glad they did it. The experience provided them with a whole new set of skills and credentials.

Create a Plan

When you truly decide that you need to find a better work situation for yourself and when you believe that the world holds other possibilities for you, options will make themselves known. When you make this mind shift, you will see opportunities that you would not have seen if you were stuck in the mode of hopelessness and helplessness. Senge describes this phenomenon in the preface to *Synchronicity*. "If we have truly committed to follow our dream, we will find that a powerful force exists beyond ourselves and our conscious will, a force that helps us along the way, nurturing our quest and transformation."[135]

I am not urging you to up and quit your job on the spot. You will definitely need to make a plan if you are considering a job change. Sara, whose story you read about earlier in the chapter, advises, "Try not to make a quick decision about leaving. See a lawyer, spend the money, and get some outside help. Even though I wanted to just walk out, I realized I had to be strong and go about it the right way."

Financial expert Suze Orman advises adults who are considering returning to college to get rid of credit card debt, make sure you will have health insurance, save extra cash, try to get more training where you are right now, and look into a 529 college savings plan, which adults can use as well as youngsters.[136]

Table 6.4 provides an opportunity to start planning a move toward a better, more satisfying work life. Your plan will need to have at least two parts to it—your goal(s) and specific things you will do to reach that goal. As you set your goals, be sure to look at the lists you made earlier in the chapter in Tables 6.1, 6.2, and 6.3 of your interests, what others see you doing, and what you really enjoy doing and want to do.

Table 6.4. My Plan

My Ultimate Job/ Career/Lifestyle Goals	What I Will Do To Achieve Them
	• _____ • _____ • _____ • _____ • _____ • _____

Books

The public library is a great place to start. Three classic books, all available on Amazon.com, can get you started:

1. *The Best Work of Your Life*

This book by Pat Alea and Patty Mullins is a must for anyone who wants to make a career change. The authors take a lightheartedly serious approach to helping you think through a career change. One of the activities that they will ask you to do is to create a timeline of your life. The timeline begins with age zero and "optimistically" ends with age one hundred. The authors invite you to plot your life on the timeline—when you were most fulfilled, what dreams you had and still have and how much time you realistically have to get going. The timeline can be a tremendous motivator to go after the life situation you want. We don't have forever.

2. *What Color Is Your Parachute? 2008: A Practical Manual for Job-Hunters and Career-Changers*
This classic resource by Richard Nelson Bolles was updated in 2008. The author makes the distinction between job changes and career changes and suggests strategies for both. Bolles also makes the point that, on average, Americans make eight job changes during their working lives. This edition includes advice on using the Internet as part of your job search strategy. A lot has changed since many of us last job hunted and this book can catch you up.

3. *Do What You Love, the Money Will Follow: Discovering Your Right Livelihood*
Author Marsha Sinetar, an organizational psychologist, left behind a secure job to do what she most enjoyed—writing, consulting, and living in the country. Sinetar offers practical advice for anyone who wants to find work that matches his or her talents and interests, such as how to deal with resistance and all the "shoulds" that can loom large when people try to find a better place for themselves in the universe She shares stories about real people that teach "how to listen to one's own self and hear one's own inner voice over the din and clatter of experts, society's expectations and media hype."[137] The book will make you feel reassured and calm and at the same time inspired to get moving with your life.

Networking

Many people find new positions through networking—finding out through someone else about a job opening or being recommended for a position. Let family and friends know you are looking and what you are hoping to find. Is there a particular office or company or store that you enjoy doing business with? Ask a few questions while you are there about what it's like to work there and if positions are opening up. What do you have to lose?

Personal Coaching

Personal life coaches are a relatively new thing. A coach can help you figure out what is most important to you, guide you in creating an action plan, and then provide ongoing support, inspiration, encouragement, and feedback as you pursue your dreams. Since anyone can hang out a sign and claim to be a life coach, be sure any coach you talk to has credentials or experience. Ask a potential coach what professional associations, such as the International Association of Coaching (IAC), he or she belongs to. A life coach without connections to any professional associations may not be sufficiently prepared to help you. Ask for names of others who have been coached by this person who will provide a reference and feedback on the coach. In the end, you will have to decide if you trust that the coach has the right experience and skills to help you. There will almost always be a fee for these services, but having another person cheering for you and helping you stay focused on your goals can help you reach them sooner and with fewer hitches.

The Power of Intention

Once you decide that, for sure, you are going to find a better working environment for yourself, one that allows you to use your talents, do your best work, live The Clover Practice™, and feel peaceful, you will have the "Power of Intention" on your side. The Power of Intention is that force described earlier as "synchronicity" where things line up, opportunities appear, and resources become available once you decide you are really going to do something about your situation.

Reflection

One thing is guaranteed to keep you stuck in a miserable job and that is doing nothing. Sometimes tactics that people say will never work end up being successful. I found a wonderful job that I held for ten years because my husband was looking through the Sunday paper classified ads. People say that looking in the want ads doesn't work. It worked for me. Buy a paper.

CONCLUSION:
LIVING THE CLOVER
PRACTICE™ EVERY DAY

Living The Clover Practice™ can make your inner life more peaceful and your work life healthier, but you will need support to really live by this practice. Consistency is the goal, not perfection, which isn't possible anyway. Here is a list of actions that should help. They are a mixed bag in terms of complexity, but each has something to offer.

1. Print out several of The Clover Practice™ bookmarks as reminders. Download from kathleenparis.com. Look at them when you get to work and whenever you have to figure out how to deal with a difficult situation. Seeing the bookmarks on your computer, in your books, and on your bulletin board will reinforce your intentions to use The Clover Practice™.

2. **Keep a daily journal of how you are doing with using The Clover Practice**™. Make a list of situations where you consciously used The Clover Practice™ and what the results were. If you slipped and weren't completely truthful, or spoke for someone else when you should not have, or got caught up in details and missed the connections, write that down too, not to beat yourself up, but to help you recognize what situations are most difficult for you. Is there a pattern of people, situations, or times of the day, when it's most difficult for you? Once you see a pattern

and know what situations are going to be hard for you, prepare for them! Then, beforehand, make special efforts to relax, give yourself a pep talk, and rehearse what you want to do or say. After a slip, relive the situation in your mind and imagine yourself handling it differently. Your awareness, by itself, can change your response to any situation. Then let it go.

3. **Take better care of your body.** You know what that means—more exercise, more fruits and vegetables. Less smoking, drinking, and stress. It's hard to be aware when we are beating up our bodies with our lifestyles.

4. **Take breaks several times a day to breathe deeply.** Many of us breathe so shallowly that we are continuously hyperventilating. This means not enough oxygen feeding our cells and too much carbon dioxide sludging them up. Use deep breathing exercises as often as you need to.

5. **Rely on more than one source of news about what's happening in the world.** We are more likely to be able to see the various truths of any situation when we regularly seek to understand through more than one lens.

6. **Put up a "Gossip-Free Zone" sign in your workspace.** Walk away when people start gossiping about others.

7. **Begin a regular practice of meditation.** Start with any book, tape, or CD by Jon Kabat-Zinn. Most communities have meditation classes through clinics or community colleges.

8. **Learn something new**—take a course in your community or online or subscribe to a new magazine on a topic that has always interested you, but you never thought you had time to explore. Our brains literally get stiff and inflexible unless we stimulate them with new stuff. And to really exchange lifelong habits for The Clover Practice™, you will need a flexible mind.

9. **Find or stay with a spiritual practice**, whether it's an organized religion or a group of like-minded people, or your own study in order to connect with the Divine in yourself and other people.

10. **If you are dealing with an addiction** (drugs, alcohol, sex, etc.) or if someone in your family is, run, don't walk, to AA or Al-Anon. See Chapter 4 for more information. Keep in mind that any addiction will affect your work. Seeking appropriate help is a sign of personal strength, not weakness. It's surprising how many people don't see it that way.

Let me leave you with a part of a Joseph Campbell poem, *The Way of the Warrior*.[138]

> The world is perfect. It's a mess.
> It has always been a mess.
> We are not going to change it.
> Our job is to straighten out
> Our own lives.

When your workplace feels crazy and confusing, you have The Clover Practice™ to fall back on. You can:

1. Tell the Truth, Always
2. Speak For Yourself
3. Declare Your Interdependence

I wish you all the best with The Clover Practice™. I hope it will help you find peace and good health in your work so you can enjoy your life.

SELECTED BIBLIOGRAPHY

Aitken, Robert. *The Mind of Clover: Essays in Zen Buddhist Ethics.* San Francisco: North Point Press, 1984.

Albom, Mitch. *Tuesdays with Morrie.* New York: Doubleday, 1997.

Alea, Pat and Patty Mullins. *The Best Work of Your Life.* New York: Perigee Press, 1998.

Arrien, Angeles. *The Four-Fold Way: Walking the Path of the Warrior, Teacher, Healer and Visionary.* New York: Harper Collins, 1993.

Babiak, Paul and Robert D. Hare. *Snakes in Suits: When Psychopaths Go to Work.* New York: HarperCollins Books, 2006.

Bakan, Joel. *The Corporation: The Pathological Pursuit of Profit and Power.* New York: Simon & Schuster, 2004.

Blanton, Brad. *Radical Honesty: How to Transform Your Life by Telling the Truth.* New York: Dell Publishing, 1996.

Bolles, Richard Nelson. *What Color Is Your Parachute? 2008: A Practical Manual for Job-Hunters and Career-Changers.* Rev. Upd. Berkeley, CA: Ten Speed Press, 2008.

Bok, Sissela. *Lying: Moral Choice in Public and Private Life.* New York: Pantheon Books, 1978.

Block, Peter. *The Answer to How Is Yes: Acting on What Matters.* San Francisco: Berrett-Koehler Publishers, 2002.

Block, Peter. *Stewardship: Choosing Service over Self-Interest.* San Francisco: Berrett-Koehler Publishers, 1996.

Bohm, David. *On Dialogue.* Edited by Lee Nichol. New York: Routledge Press, 1996.

Callahan, David. *The Cheating Culture: Why More Americans Are Doing Wrong to Get Ahead.* Orlando: Harcourt Inc., 2004.

Campbell, Joseph. *Reflections on the Art of Living: A Joseph Campbell Companion.* Edited by Diane K. Osbon. San Anselmo, CA: The Joseph Campbell Foundation, 1991.

Canfield, Jack and Mark Victor Hansen. *The Aladdin Factor.* New York: The Berkley Publishing Group, 1995.

Capra, Fritjof. *The Web of Life.* New York: Doubleday, 1996.

Cutright, Layne and Paul Cutright. *You're Never Upset for the Reason You Think: The Cure for the Common Upset.* Las Vegas: Heart to Heart International, 2004.

Dyer, Wayne W. *The Power of Intention: Learning to Co-Create Your World Your Way.* Carlsbad, CA: Hay House, Inc., 2004.

Fairtlough, Gerard. *The Three Ways of Getting Things Done: Hierarchy, Heterarchy & Responsible Autonomy in Organizations: International Edition.* Devon, UK: Triarchy Press, 2007.

Gray, Elizabeth Dodson. *Patriarchy As a Conceptual Trap.* Wellesley, MA: Roundtable Press, 1973.

Hanh, Thich Nhat. *Peace Is Every Step: The Path of Mindfulness in Everyday Life.* New York: Bantam Books, 1991.

Hannegan, Eileen. *Your Truth: Know It, Speak It, Live It: A Guide for People Seeking Authenticity in Their Personal and Professional Lives.* New York: MJF Books, 1996.

Jarow, Rick. *Creating the Work You Love: Courage, Commitment and Career.* Rochester, Vermont: Inner Traditions, 1995.

Jaworski, Joseph. *Synchronicity.* San Francisco: Berrett-Koehler Publishers, 1996.

Kabat-Zinn, Jon. *Full Catastrophe Living: Using the Wisdom of Your Body and Mind to Face Stress, Pain, and Illness.* New York: Dell, 1990.

Kabat-Zinn, Jon. *Wherever You Go, There You Are: Mindfulness Meditation in Everyday Life.* New York: Hyperion, 1994.

Kegan, Robert and Lisa Laskow Lahey. *How the Way We Talk Can Change the Way We Work.* San Francisco: Jossey-Bass, 2001.

Kelly, Marjorie. *The Divine Right of Capital: Dethroning the Corporate Aristocracy.* Berrett-Koehler Publishers, 2001.

Lerner, Harriet. *Fear and Other Uninvited Guests: Tackling the Anxiety, Fear, and Shame That Keeps Us from Optimal Living and Loving.* New York: HarperCollins, 2004.

Lulic, Margaret A. *Who We Could Be at Work.* Boston: Butterworth-Heinemann, 1996.

Lucas, James R. *Fatal Illusions: Shedding a Dozen Unrealities That Can Keep Your Organization From Success.* New York: American Management Association, 1997.

Nyberg, David. *The Varnished Truth: Truth Telling and Deceiving in Ordinary Life.* Chicago: University of Chicago Press, 1993.

Pagano, Barbara and Elizabeth Pagano. *The Transparency Edge: How Credibility Can Make or Break You in Business.* Chicago: McGraw-Hill, 2004.

Patterson, Kerry, Joseph Grenny, Ron McMillan, and Al Switzler. *Crucial Conversations: Tools for Talking When the Stakes Are High.* Chicago: McGraw-Hill, 2002.

Pennebaker, James, W. *Opening Up: The Healing Power of Expressing Emotions.* 2d. ed. New York: Guilford Press, 1997.

Roach, Michael. *The Diamond Cutter: The Buddha on Managing Your Business and Your Life.* New York: Doubleday, 2003.

Ruiz, Don Miguel. *The Four Agreements: A Practical Guide to Personal Wisdom.* San Rafael, CA: Amber-Allen Publishing, 1997.

Ryan, Kathleen D., Daniel K. Oestreich, and George A. Orr III. *The Courageous Messenger: How to Successfully Speak Up at Work.* San Francisco: Jossey-Bass, 1996.

Ryan, Kathleen D., Daniel K. Oestreich. *Driving Fear Out of the Workplace: Creating the High-Trust, High-Performance Organization.* San Francisco: Jossey-Bass, 1998.

Schultz, Will. *The Truth Option.* Berkeley, CA: 10 Speed Press, 1984.

Sheehy, Gail. *New Passages: Mapping Your Life across Time.* New York: Ballantine Books, 1995.

Sinetar, Marsha. *Do What You Love, The Money Will Follow: Discovering Your Right Livelihood.* New York: Dell Publishing, 1987.

Stone, Douglas, Bruce Patton, and Shila Heen. *Difficult Conversations: How to Discuss What Matters Most.* New York: Penguin Books, 1999.

Tolle, Eckhart. *The Power of Now: A Guide to Spiritual Enlightenment.* Novalto, CA: New World Library, 1999.

Tolle, Eckhart. *A New Earth: Awakening to Your Life's Purpose.* New York: PLUME, 2005.

Warren, Rick. *The Purpose Driven Life: What On Earth Am I Here For?* Grand Rapids, MI: Zondervan, 2002.

Margaret Wheatley. *Leadership and the New Science: Discovering Order in a Chaotic World.* San Francisco: Berrett-Koehler Publishers, 1999.

Whitmyer, Claude, ed. *Mindfulness and Mindful Work: Explorations in Right Livelihood.* Berkeley: Parallax Press, 1994.

ENDNOTES

1 Peter Block, *The Answer to How is Yes* (San Francisco: Berrett-Koehler, 2002), 169.

2 U.S. Public Health Service. *Mental Health: A Report of the Surgeon General* 1999. http://www.surgeongeneral.gov/library/mentalhealth/chapter1/sec1.html#mental_points.

3 Answers.com: Health http://www.answers.com/topic/mental-health.

4 Robert Aitken, *The Mind of Clover: Essays in Zen Buddhist Ethics* (San Francisco: North Point Press, 1984), 68.

5 June Kronholz, "Adultery: Is honesty the best policy?" *The Wall Street Journal.* Reprinted in *The Standard-Times* (1998), http://www.southcoasttoday.com/daily/02-98/02-06-98/b01li054.htm/.

6 Nan DeMars, "Taking the Ethics Pulse," Office Ethics Columns [n.d.], http://www.office-ethics.com/officecolumns/ethicspulse.html.

7 Barbara Pagano and Elizabeth Pagano, *The Transparency Edge: How Credibility Can Make or Break You in Business* (Chicago: McGraw-Hill, 2004), 18.

8 Ibid.

9 Ron Suskind, "Without a Doubt," *NYT Magazine* (October 17, 2004), http://www.nytimes.com/2004/10/17/magazine/17BUSH.html.

10 Amey Stone, [blog] December 14, 2006, http://www.blog-gingstocks.com/2006/12/14/best-and-worst-enrons-ugly-end-game-skillings-sentencing-lay/.

11   Penelope Patsuris, "The Corporate Scandal Sheet," *Forbes. com* (August 26, 2002), http://www.forbes.com/2002/07/25/accountingtracker.html.

12 Clint Willis and Nate Hardcastle, *The I Hate Corporate America Reader: How Big Companies from McDonald's to Microsoft Are Destroying Our Way of Life* (New York: Thunder's Mouth Press, 2004), 18.

13 Joel Bakan, *The Corporation: The Pathological Pursuit of Profit and Power* (New York: Simon & Schuster, 2004), 123.

14 Willis and Hardcastle, *The I Hate Corporate America Reader*, 48.

15 David Nyberg, *The Varnished Truth: Truth Telling and Deceiving in Ordinary Life* (Chicago: The University of Chicago Press, 1993), 25.

16 Mitch Albom, *Tuesdays with Morrie* (New York: Doubleday, 1997), 36.

17 Eckhart Tolle, *A New Earth: Awakening to Your Life's Purpose* (New York: PLUME, 2005), 22.

18 Peter Block, *Stewardship: Choosing Service over Self-Interest* (San Francisco: Berrett-Koehler, 1996), 93.

19 Tom Sant, *Messages that Matter* [n.d.], http://www.santcorp.com/best_practices/mtm.htm.

20 Nan DeMars. *You Want Me to Do What?: When, Where, and How to Draw the Line at Work* (New York: Fireside, 1998), 21.

21 Allison Kornet, "The Truth About Lying," *Psychology Today* (May/June, 1997), 52.

22 Ibid., 55.

23 James Pennebaker, *Opening Up: The Healing Power of Expressing Emotions* (New York: Guildford Press, 1997), 36-7.

24 Eileen R. Hannegan, *Your Truth: Know It, Speak It, Live It: A Guide for People Seeking Authenticity in Their Personal and Professional Lives* (New York: MJF Books, 1996), 51.

25 Ibid., 66.

26 Peter M. Senge, *The Fifth Discipline: The Art and Practice of the Learning Organization* (New York: Doubleday, 1990), 174-204.

27 Geshe Michael Roach, *The Diamond Cutter* (New York: Doubleday, 2000), 103.

28 Ibid.

29 Margaret Wheatley, *Leadership and the New Science: Discovering Order in a Chaotic World* (San Francisco: Berrett-Koehler Publishers, 1999), 37.

30 "Guiding Principles," Rotary International, http://www.rotary.org/en/AboutUs/RotaryInternational/Guiding Principles/Pages/ridefault.aspx

31 Hannegan, *Your Truth*, 93.

32 Kathleen D. Ryan and Daniel K. Oestreich, *Driving Fear out of the Workplace: Creating the High-Trust, High-Performance Organization*, 2d ed. (San Francisco: Jossey-Bass Publishers, 1998), 6.

33 Hannegan, *Your Truth*, 3.

34 Robert Kegan and Lisa Laskow Lahey, *How the Way We Talk Can Change the Way We Work: Seven Languages for Transformation* (San Francisco: Jossey-Bass, 2001), 67-68.

35 Ibid.

36 Hannegan, *Your Truth*, 24.

37 Ibid., 13.

38 Al Kaltman, *Cigars, Whiskey, and Winning: Leadership Lessons from General Ulysses S. Grant* (New York: Prentice Hall, 1998), 14.

39 Kegan and Lahey, *How the Way We Talk Can Change the Way We Work*, 128.

40 Kerry Patterson, Joseph Grenny, Ron McMillan, and Al Switzler, *Crucial Conversations: Tools for Talking When Stakes Are High* (New York: McGraw-Hill, 2002), 9.

41 Grant Wiggins, "Assessment as Feedback," *New Horizons for Learning* (March 2004), http://www.newhorizons.org/strategies/assess/wiggins.htm.

42 Patterson et al., *Crucial Conversations*, 124.

43 Ibid., 101.

44 Ibid.

45 Ibid., 131-133.

46 Ibid., 132.

47 Paul Babiak and Robert Hare, *Snakes in Suits: When Psychopaths go to Work* (New York: HarperCollins, 2006), 301.

48 Rob Sandelin, *Community Resource Guide* (1997), http://www.ic.org/nica/Process/Relation.html.

49 Robert Bacal, "Facing Down Workplace Gossip," Office of Employee Assistance, Florida International University, 2003, http://www.fiu.edu/~oea/InsightsFall2004/online_library/articles/facing%20down%20workplace%20gossip.htm.

50 Ibid.

51 Kathleen D. Ryan, Daniel K. Oestreich, George A. Orr III, *The Courageous Messenger: How To Successfully Speak Up at Work* (San Francisco: Jossey-Bass Publishers, 1996), 65.

52 Hannegan, *Your Truth*, 67.

53 Ibid., 65.

54 *Nietzsche Circle,* http://www.nietzschecircle.com/nietzsche_work.html.

55 *Meditations of John Muir: Nature's Temple,* Chris Highland, ed. (Berkeley, CA: Wilderness Press, 2001), 63.

56 Claus Otto Scharmer, *Every Institution is a Living System,* conversation with Arie de Geus (London, September 22, 1999), http://www.dialogonleadership.org/deGeus-1999.html.

57 Fritjof Capra, *The Web of Life* (New York: Doubleday, 1996), 28.

58 Robert Aitken, *The Mind of Clover: Essays in Zen Buddhist Ethics* (San Francisco: North Point Press, 1984), 19.

59 "Can Chrysler Survive Another Crisis?" *Society of Manufacturing Engineers,* January 30, 2001, http://www.sme.org/cgi-bin/get-press.pl?&&20011304&ND&&SME&.

60 Wheatley, *Leadership and the New Science,* 30.

61 Capra, *The Web of Life,* 11.

62 Wayne W. Dyer, *The Power of Intention: Learning How to Co-create Your World Your Way* (Carlsbad, CA: Hay House, Inc., 2004), 205.

63 Layne Cutright and Paul Cutright, *You're Never Upset for the Reason You Think,* 2d ed. (Las Vegas, NV: Heart to Heart, 2008), 8-9.

64 Thich Nhat Hanh, *Peace is Every Step: The Path of Mindfulness in Everyday Life* (New York: Bantam Books, 1991), 95.

65 Ibid., 96.

66 Albom, *Tuesdays with Morrie,* 155.

67 Marsha Sinetar, *Do What You Love, The Money Will Follow: Discovering Your Right Livelihood* (New York: Dell Publishing, 1987), 25.

68 Ibid., p. 27.

69 Arthur Schopenhauer, Archive for 'Arthur Schopenhauer' [n.d.] http://favouritequotations.ca/category/arthur-schopenhauer/.

70 Cutright, Paul and Layne Cutright, "Radical Personal Responsibility," in *Earthling Communication.* http://www.earthlingcommunication.com/a/self-understanding/accepting-personal-responsibility.php.

71 Aviel Goodman, "Addiction: definition and implications," *British Journal of Addiction* 85 (1990): 1404.

72 Angeles Arrien, *The Four-Fold Way: Walking the Path of the the Warrior, Teacher, Healer and Visionary* (New York: Harper Collins, 1993), 67.

73 "Alcoholism Statistics," http://addiction.lovetoknow.com/wiki/Alcoholism_Statistics.

74 Aitken, *The Mind of Clover*, 18.

75 "Alcoholism Statistics," http://addiction.lovetoknow.com/wiki/Alcoholism_Statistics.

76 Maya Angelou, Wikiquote, http://en.wikiquote.org/wiki/Maya_Angelou.

77 Elizabeth Gilbert, *Eat, Pray, Love: One Woman's Search for Everything Across Italy, India and Indonesia* (*New York, Penguin Books, 2007*), 206.

78 The failure rate of large companies is not only surprisingly high, but it is also accelerating according to *Long Term Success or Survival.* Innovation Zen, http://innovationzen.com/blog/2006/07/22/long-term-success-or-survival/.

79 Ken Blanchard and Jesse Stoner, "The Vision Thing: Without It You'll Never Be a World-Class Organization," *Leader to Leader*, 31 (Winter 2004), http://www.leadertoleader.org/knowledge-center/journal.aspx?ArticleID=74.

80 Tom Peters and Robert Waterman, *In Search of Excellence: Lessons from America's Best-Run Companies* (New York: HarperCollins, 1982), 235.

81 Marjorie Kelly, *The Divine Right of Capital: Dethroning the Corporate Aristocracy* (San Francisco: Berrett-Koehler Publishers, 2001), 3.

82 Ibid., 6.

83 It is not unusual for nonprofit boards to meet for strategic planning without any staff or clientele beyond the executive director. They are willing to plan in the absence of what the people in the trenches know about the groups they serve. These organizations are copying (needlessly) corporate practices based on the belief that those at the top know everything they need to know to guide the organization into the future.

84 Block, *Stewardship*, 7.

85 Elizabeth Dodson Gray, *Patriarchy as a Conceptual Trap* (Wellesley, MA: Routable Press, 1982), 47.

86 Ibid., 17.

87 Frederick Winslow Taylor, *Principles of Scientific Management* (Sioux Falls, SD: NuVision Publications, 2007), 63.

88 Robert Kanigel, *The One Best Way: Frederick Winslow Taylor and the Enigma of Efficiency* (New York: Penguin Books. 1997), 7.

89 Block, *Stewardship*, 8.

90 Peter Block "Accountability & Commitment" (December 7, 2005), The Hunter Conference on Quality, Madison, WI.

91 Parker J. Palmer, "The New Professional: The Aims of Education Revisited," *Change* 39 (November/December 2007):11-12.

92 Block, *Stewardship*, 18.

93 Joel Henning in Peter Block, *Stewardship: Choosing Service over Self-Interest* (San Francisco: Berrett-Koehler, 1996), xii.

94 Paul Kaihla, "Getting inside the Boss's Head," *Business 2.0* (November 2003), http://money.cnn.com/magazines/business2/business2_archive/2003/11/01/351936/index.htm.

95 Ibid.

96 Paul Babiak and Robert Hare, *Snakes in Suits: When Psychopaths go to Work* (New York: HarperCollins, 2006), 19.

97 Ibid., xi-xiii.

98 Block, *Stewardship*, 45.

99 Ibid.

100 James R. Lucas, *Fatal Illusions: Shedding a Dozen Unrealities That Can Keep Your Organization from Success* (American Management Association: Chicago, 1997), 1.

101 Ibid., 2.

102 George Bernard Shaw, http://thinkexist.com/quotation/the_single_biggest_problem_in_communication_is/155222.html.

103 Steve Denning, http://www.stevedenning.com/communications_viewpoint.html.

104 Lucas, *Fatal Illusions*, 134.

105 Wheatley, *Leadership and the New Science*, 18-19.

106 "Fewer Employers Forbid Talking about Pay; HRnext.com Survey Shows Many Employers View Issue as Hot Potato," BNET Business Network (April 4, 2001), http://findarticles.com/p/articles/mi_m0EIN/is_2001_April_4/ai_72727120.

107 "Pay Confidentiality Policies under Siege," HRnext.com (2000), http://www.vault.com/nr/ newsmain.jsp?nr_page=3&ch_id=401&article_id=52110&cat_id=1090.

108 Tolle, *A New Earth*, 28.

109 Lucas, *Fatal Illusions*, 28.

110 Elizabeth Scott. "Chronic Job Stress is a Risk Factor for Heart Disease," About.com (2008), http://stress.about.com/od/stresshealth/a/jobstress.htm.

111 "How Stress Affects the Immune System," About.com: Mental Health (November 6, 2005), http://mentalhealth.about.com/od/stress/a/stressimmune604.htm.

112 Lancaster University Management School, "Research reveals that dissatisfaction at work causes illness" (18 November 2005), http://www.lums.lancs.ac.uk/news/cooperresearch/.

113 Joseph Campbell, The Quotations Page, http://www.quotationspage.com/quote/4015.html.

114 Richard Nelson Bolles, *What Color Is Your Parachute? 2008: A Practical Manual for Job-Hunters and Career-Changers*, Rev. Upd. (Berkeley, CA: Ten Speed Press; 2008), 22.

115 Sinetar, *Do What You Love*, 51.

116 Margaret A. Lulic, *Who We Could Be at Work*. rev. (Boston: Butterworth-Heinemann, 1996), 1.

117 Sinetar, *Do What You Love*, 10-11.

118 Brian Tracy, "Finding Your True Calling," http://www.nightingaleconant.co.uk/AE_Article.aspx? i=260&article=FindingYourTrueCalling&dloc=2.

119 Genesis 3:16, *The Bible*, New International Version.

120 Kahlil Gibran, *The Prophet* (New York: Alfred A. Knopf, 1923), 28.

121 Albom, *Tuesdays with Morrie*, 43.

122 Alan M. Weber, "Is Your Job Your Calling?" (extended interview) Fast Company, 13 (January, 1998), 108, http://www.fastcompany.com/magazine/13/hbrplus.html.

123 Ibid.

124 Rick Jarow, *Creating the Work You Love Workshop*, http://anticareer.com/concept.html#sevensteps.

125 Rick Jarow, *"Intro to the Work,"* The Alchemy of Abundance: Opening to Life's Fullness with Rick Jarow, http://alchemyofabundance.wordpress.com/intro-to-the-work/.

126 Jarow, *Creating the Work You Love Workshop*.

127 Rick Jarow, *The Anti Career Webpage*, http://anticareer.com/concept.html.

128 Tracy, "Finding Your True Calling," http://www.nightingaleconant.co.uk/AE_Article.aspx?i=260& article=FindingYourTrueCalling&dloc=2.

129 Alan Deutschman, "Change or Die," *Fast Company*, (May, 2005), 54.

130 Ibid., 55.

131 Libby Sander, "Blue-Collar Boomers Take Work Ethnic to College." *Chronicle of Higher Education*, 54
(January 18, 2008), A13.

132 Ibid., A21.

133 Rick Jarow, "Guidance from the Goddess," Reprinted from *New Age Journal*, [n.d.], http://www.anticareer.com/guidancegoddess.html.

134 Angus Loten, "Immigrant Startups Continue to Grow," *Inc.com* (May 23, 2007), http://www.inc.com/news/articles/200705/startups.html.

135 Peter Senge in Joseph Jaworski, *Synchronicity* (San Francisco: Berrett-Koehler Publishers, 1996), xi.

136 Suze Orman, "Getting Set to Start Over," O: *The Oprah Magazine*, February 2007, 66.

137 Sinetar, *Do What You Love*, p. 6.

138 Joseph Campbell, *Reflections on the Art of Living: A Joseph Campbell Companion*, ed. Diane K. Osbon (San Anselmo, CA: The Joseph Campbell Foundation: 1991), 17.

ABOUT THE AUTHOR

Kathleen A. Paris holds a PhD in educational administration from the University of Wisconsin-Madison. She is a distinguished consultant emeritus for the Office of Quality Improvement and lecturer in the Department of Educational Leadership and Policy Analysis at UW-Madison. For over twenty years, she has provided management consulting services for education, business, and non-profit organizations. Paris received the Wisconsin Governor's Export Achievement award in 1990. The author's award-winning web site on effective meetings has gained national and international attention. See kathleenparis.com.

)